A Dog

Peggy

The Life and Times of a
Rescued Greyhound

Clare Cogbill

DEDICATION

For all racing greyhounds across the world, may there soon come a day when you will no longer have to race for your life, when you will know the comfort of a duvet spread across a sofa, and the kindness of a person saying to you 'Good dog... let's go home.'

... and Alun and Connor for sharing my absolute love of dogs

CONTENTS

ACKNOWLEDGMENTS

To those of you who love animals as I do – we really can make the lives of dogs and all animals better. Together we are strong.

To those who encourage me, inspire me, and love me despite my idiosyncrasies, I thank you!

Thank you, as well, to those who have read my words and given me your valuable feedback, I am humbled by your generosity of spirit. To Connor McMorran for the wonderful cover – yet again I am extremely grateful.

But most of all I thank Peggy and her comrades Ralph and Lucy, for constantly entertaining (especially Lucy, who takes her terrier duties very seriously), and always being an inspiration to me.

Introduction

A book about a special dog – a special relationship with a special dog, that is – will generally finish up with the canine protagonist's unfortunate demise. Dogs don't live as long as most humans do, and that is the key, regrettable fact of the deep, reciprocal human-dog bond we have forged over thousands of years.

This book, however, begins in this introduction with telling you about the ending by letting you know that Peggy will be okay. I hope this will allow you to not feel sad in anticipation that the end might be nigh for Peggy. She's not gone. No, not at all, she's still very much here with us. Her sleek, black hairs are turning whiter, seemingly by the day and giving her that air of an all-knowing aged dog, but she's still our cheeky, pointy-faced canine.

Her joints are not what they once were, but they are being assisted by flaxseed omega oil capsules, veterinary-prescribed painkilling medication, a healthy diet, and a magnetic collar which works on the same theory as those magnetic bracelets worn by arthritic people. Due to these ageing joints, and as an ex-racer the inevitable residual problems from her old racing injuries, she sometimes seems

1

a little slower than she used to be, yet she is still the Peggy we have known and loved since she came into our lives back in 2011.

Yes, indeed, she's still very much making her presence known, just as she's always done. She is a greyhound, yes, and she does have pretty much all of those anticipated greyhound traits, especially in loving the sofa and spending hours on end lying on her back with her four legs stretched up towards the sky. She's not fussy about whether the sofa has lots of scatter cushions, they apparently do fine to prop yourself against, or even if the sofa is empty, bar a throw to keep it clean. When sofas are empty like that they simply provide maximum space for greyhounds to stretch out their long body and, of course, all four of those aforementioned long limbs.

Peggy also loves treats, and on each treat-occasion she likes to select which one she's going to have – usually choosing the largest and most expensive of the options available to her. And, similar to some greyhounds (but definitely not all), she unfortunately dislikes cats. With a passion!

Despite their sometimes bad press regarding their relationships with people's feline friends, not all greyhounds dislike cats, but Peggy just happens to be typical of one of those greyhounds who does.

She's now twelve years old. I decided, for the sake of this book, to check out the expected lifespan of a greyhound. Most suggest it to be between ten and twelve years. Twelve? But she's already twelve and doesn't look or seem as though she's going anywhere anytime soon! I found one estimation which said that greyhounds sometimes live to be up to fifteen. It would be nice to think that we'll have her around for a good while longer, just so long as she remains in good health (albeit supported by pain relief for her old racing injuries), and is happily doing what happy greyhounds do. Apart from her dodgy limbs, there's nothing else physically wrong with her – she's in 'pretty good nick', as they say, whoever 'they' might be.

And, anyway, Peggy has to stay around for some time yet because she has to tell her story, and then be able to spend time reveling in the glory of being a canine author – just like her adopted canine companions, gentle giant Ralph, and the little dog with the teeth, Lucy-Luella.

It's important to tell her story as it happened, and I imagine for this she needs your understanding. As you'd expect, she doesn't really talk! However often I've looked into those velvet-brown eyes and wished she would whisper even a few soft words about how she's doing, it unfortunately remains a fact that we humans and our dogs have to find other methods of effective communication. And it can be incredibly difficult to know whether we've got it right: Is she happy? Have we done okay by her? Does she really want one of those particular treat options? Or is there something else on her wish list she'd prefer to have? I think, though, that with Peggy the grass is always greener, and in her mind there will definitely be another piece of food which is tastier than the one in front of her, or indeed, the one she's just eaten!

So, no, unfortunately she doesn't really talk and, naturally, she doesn't write – if she did then I imagine she would have been the subject of some awful invasive experiment and never have crossed our path. Peggy's story is, however, fairly typical of many rescued greyhounds. She really is one of the luckier ones, and the story she tells here might not always be the story of her *own* life, but the story she's likely seen happening to other greyhounds around her – to other dogs who perhaps didn't end up being quite as lucky as she's been.

I obviously can't know for sure whether the things she's experienced are those I've included in the first part of the book, which reflects on her racing days, but what I (we) describe happening is happening all the time to greyhounds in the UK, and in many other countries around the world, so it's therefore important to convey that.

The greyhound industry is notoriously rife with cruelty. There are far more dogs born than are ever used on the track, and this mass over-production of dogs results in the immeasurable (because the fate of all dogs is not accounted for) subsequent killing of many greyhounds each year. In race kennels some dogs are housed singly, some with other greyhounds, and some of them are permanently muzzled whilst in kennels. I don't know whether Peggy was ever one of those dogs – I prefer to think that she wasn't, because I really want to believe that nothing terrible ever happened to her. But in my heart I know that all my optimism about her past can't be true.

For this book I have assumed Peggy was kenneled with another greyhound, and I (we) have named that greyhound Roxy. Roxy represents the greyhound friendships that must be forged by the dogs who live these awful lives; the temporary connections they make along the way, which perhaps provide them with some level of companionship. Hopefully for the few lucky ones there will eventually be a loving forever home in which they can form permanent bonds. Conversely, for the less lucky greyhounds there will be a fate awaiting them of cruel treatment followed by an early death.

Peggy has a penchant for surrounding herself with soft toys and carrying them around in her mouth – just in the way that a bitch would carry her offspring. While I'm sure from information I've been able to find out about her that she's never had puppies, the maternal instinct in her is strong. This is to the extent that when we once used an appeasing pheromone spray on our nervous lurcher Ralph's bed to make him feel less anxious, we didn't get the chance to see whether it was going to help him, because the pheromones drove Peggy absolutely wild with expressions of maternal behaviours. She immediately began nesting – desperately raking at the bed and circling in it to make a nest for herself, while she panted and panted. It was as though her hormones were telling her to nest because she was certain those puppies (the ones she definitely wasn't having because at the time she was already neutered) would be produced at any minute!

Abandoning the idea of using pheromones to help Ralph, we quickly thoroughly washed all the bedding that had been sprayed. Instead we searched elsewhere to find other solutions to help him with his problems. In the end, though, with Ralph it was simply time and patience that were the keys to his recovery from the awful life he'd had before. We're pretty sure his past involved being an illegal hare coursing dog, and he somehow managed to escape from the menace of the people and community into which he was born. We suspect Ralph's puppyhood was similar to Peggy's in a socially isolated kennels, but he has additionally without a doubt encountered people from the pits of society; people whose default position is in harming animals.

The majority of racing dogs spend much of their time in stark, bleak, sometimes parasite-ridden kennels, and many experience harsh training methods. Some dogs are illegally injected with steroids and other drugs in an attempt to make them run faster, and many bitches are injected with hormones to delay or prevent their heat. All of these drugs have potential long-term health consequences for the dogs involved.

As they race around the track the dogs frequently

suffer severe injuries due to the way the tracks are designed – the track's layout is often not an easy, smooth run. Once injured, the dogs are no longer any use, and some, like Peggy, will be handed over to a rescue organization. Many, however, along with the surplus slower greyhounds who didn't make it to the track in the first place, simply fall off the grid – never to be seen again; while some others meet their premature end in a veterinary surgery.

Some surplus dogs are sold to other countries and then transported thousands of miles as far away as China or Australia. The conditions in some countries can be even worse for greyhounds than those in the UK. After a successful racing 'career' of their own, faster dogs are either kept as breeding bitches, or, if male, as stud dogs or sperm 'donors'. This sperm is then used for artificial insemination of the recipient bitch – and all in the desperate attempt to produce another potential winner.

And amid all this destruction and disappearance of thousands of dogs, people are suffering too, mostly from problems such as gambling. Gambling has the potential for causing severe financial problems, and consequently the sad breakdown of families caught up in such difficulties.

I think that because I have the opinions I have about animal abuse, I can't imagine why anyone would support an industry such as this one, particularly when it is common knowledge that it's such an awful deal for greyhounds. Many who bet on these dogs will know what goes on because they will see signs of the horror all the time. Yet, still, they turn a blind eye and continue to support it.

A change in mindset needs to take place so these dogs are no longer subject to racing – the legislation that exists certainly does little to protect them. Making it completely illegal will mean that, for the most part, it will go away. If managed carefully, the dogs who are currently racing will be assisted by rescue charities in finding their way to a life in a forever home – just in the way that dogs like Peggy have. I don't think that's an unreasonable dream. I believe it's something that has to be done so we humans can establish a relationship with all greyhounds as one of compassion.

On a personal level, and with this being the third in a sort-of-trilogy of books about Ralph, Peggy and Lucy, I don't know why these three particular dogs have inspired me to write about them. There have been so many other dogs in my life, each with their own story. Perhaps it's that this trio of dogs entered my life at a time when I was ready to tell the tales of the problems that are rife in the world of dogs, and at a point when I felt the need to write about this important human-animal bond. It's possible that after this I won't write any more dog books, and shall instead concentrate on other projects I have in the pipeline. But, you never know, sometime in the future another dog may come along who inspires me to tell their story.

In the meantime, I ask you to just go along with what Peggy has to say, to let any prejudices about the concept of talking dogs slide away, and get into the moment – into Peggy's moment. She really is a bit of a character, and I hope I have done her justice. I also ask you to go along with her descriptions of the bad times, safe in the knowledge that she will be okay. What she's seen and experienced as a racing dog is sometimes awful, and adds weight to a call for dog racing to be banned.

And so, if we could reach inside Peggy's mind and extract her memories, if we could glean from her some information about the 'lot' of a racing greyhound, and in her case one who was lucky enough to be rescued, then perhaps what follows in this book – her book – is what she'd say:

A Dog Like Peggy

PART ONE

EARLY TIMES

Over to Peggy...

Chapter One

Life in a Little World

They (humans, that is) talk about the innate things that young animals do which are so instinctive you just do them, basically because nature tells you what you need to do. When we mammal creatures are born, baby human creatures included I would imagine, we are driven towards finding warmth, finding food, and responding to the care and attention provided by the one who gave birth to us.

I don't remember my birth, I suppose not many of us do, but I would imagine it was a rather traumatic experience, with blood, other body fluids, and lots of gore. Even though each individual's birth is unique to them: every dog; every cat (I'm not really a fan); every sheep; every bird; every human, then perhaps it really is best that we block out something quite as disturbing as having to be born. The thought blows my canine mind when I think about it too deeply.

If I'm entirely honest, I don't remember much about those early days at all, only that I vaguely recall there was something inside me which was driving me to be competitive. When one of my siblings would try to shove me out of the way so they could reach the warmest places right next to our mother's belly, or when one of them nuzzled me out of the way when I was trying to suckle, I would push back harder. I wouldn't do this in a nasty way, of course, just in a polite way which showed them I could look after myself! I didn't want more than my share; I just wanted to make sure I got what I needed. Clare tells me it was probably this trait that made me thrive – something about a guy named Darwin from the 1800s and the fittest surviving, or something like that.

I have a vague recollection of someone hurting my ear when I was very young, I can remember squealing, and that there was a strange scent of something I later learned had come from inside my body – blood. Later on, and especially in my racing years, humans would often flick back my ear to see something in there; it was almost as though they could read what they saw. I wasn't so sure I liked being identified by whatever they saw in my ear. After all, even then I had a perfectly respectable name.

I don't remember exactly how many of us there were snuggled against our mother's belly – quite a lot, I think. One little brother of mine they called 'the runt' died when we were very young. Perhaps if they hadn't called him a runt he'd have tried a bit harder to survive. They could have been a bit more helpful and given him a bit of extra food to help him along a bit. But, no, he had to compete with the rest of us.

It wasn't so cozy in that building I was born in. We only had one rug and some newspaper between all of us, and when daytime changed to dark outside, dimness accompanied the quiet of the night. Now, we dogs are known for using our noses much more than our eyes, but we greyhounds are sight hounds, so we do actually see very well. Not then, though, we couldn't see properly until we were a bit older, so all the time we relied on our instincts to drive us toward what we needed – and the only thing we needed then was our mother.

In the kennels around us were other greyhound mums with their own litters of pups. There was a lot of squeaking and puppy murmurings coming from each of the kennels, each young animal taking comfort in the care and love received from their own mother.

17

In hindsight, I think that on the whole those were contented days, despite the damp and the cold. I felt a deep bond with my mother and loved it when she licked my face, and then flipped me over to wash my nether parts. I was secure and safe. Back then we didn't know any different. Once we were parted from one another I wasn't to find that sense of security and safety for a long time into the future.

In those early days we didn't often leave the kennels. We'd left that once on the occasion of the sore ears, and then some time later when we were all placed in a box, taken outside, and then placed on the ground. A man picked us up, rubbed his big, rough hands along our sides, and then peered deeply into our eyes.

We were then all put into a grassy field. I felt free for the first time ever and was gamboling over and over with my brothers and sisters. One of the humans encouraged us all to chase him, and I found myself running alongside my sister, a white dog with grey patches. And then our brother overtook us. He was striped brown and black. The three of us were put back into the box and the rest of our siblings were put into another box. I never found out what became of them. They simply disappeared and we never saw them again.

When we got back to the kennel, just the three of us, our mother sniffed around us. She wouldn't leave us alone. She went up to the gate and whimpered, and then she began to make a sound I'd never before heard her make. She howled and howled. It was the loudest and most disturbing noise I'd ever heard in my short life.

But then other mothers from the block joined her in her sorrow, and they all chorused the most bloodcurdling sounds from deep in their throats. Recalling it now sends shivers down my long greyhound spine.

Later on when she was utterly exhausted she came and snuggled down next to us, her three remaining pups, and we reciprocated all the love she'd ever given us by snuggling into her like we'd never done before.

The following day she was taken away from us and, just like our siblings, we never saw her again.

Chapter Two

Sisters

Just as our mother had grieved over her missing pups, when she was taken away, so, too, the three of us grieved and whimpered and whined. We had only the one very dirty and smelly rug between us, our kennel reeked of our waste, and the three of us snuggled against one another for comfort – seeking solace from each other's warmth. We washed one another just like our mother had washed us, and we eagerly waited for her return. But she never came. Some others in the block still had their mother in with them, and we felt ourselves longing for such reassurance and protection.

Each day someone came and cleaned out our kennels and shook the rug. Sometimes they even gave us fresh newspaper. We had food put in our bowls just once a day, and each afternoon we were taken into the field to run.

And didn't we run? Didn't we just.

We ran every day, sometimes three or four times, and each time we had to race around the field chasing bags, toys, sometimes just one another. I liked to run, but sometimes when it was hot I would rather have been in the cold kennel. The building wasn't comfortable, but the heat was sometimes intolerable.

We didn't only run with one another, sometimes the dogs from the other kennels were outside at the same time and we ran with them. The three of us were getting taller and, it seemed, longer. My tail was long and thin, and when I ran I held it in line with my spine.

Each day I would also be taken out into the field on my own with the humans. Round and round the field I would run, sometimes many times. And then I'd stop. Panting and panting I'd wait in desperation for them to put me back inside, but then they chased me and made me run some more.

When the point of exhaustion came, they would take me into a room beyond the kennel block. In the corner was a machine and they used to stand me on it, attaching my rope to a bar above the machine so I couldn't get away. Suddenly the floor would begin to move and all I could do was walk. And then the floor would move faster and faster until I was running. I don't know for how long I was on that machine each time, but I hated it. I was frightened, and I longed for the freedom of the field, or to be in the kennel with my two siblings.

That machine was part of a regular routine, and as I got older it felt as though I was on it for longer and longer. I tried to pull away each time they put me on it. But they were stronger than I was – a lot stronger. I was exhausted and sometimes I'd squeal to tell them to let me stop, but they forced me to keep on running. It seemed as though the more I ran, the farther and faster they wanted me to go. But I wasn't running anywhere. Just on the spot on the machine I despised so much.

I don't know whether my siblings had to run on the machine, I think they did, because sometimes I thought I could sense fear and exhaustion on them when they were put back in the kennels.

And then, one day, just as my other siblings and mother had disappeared, so did my black and brown stripy brother. There was only the two of us left – just my white and blue-grey sister and me. Her name was Roxy. The two of us used to snuggle together, one of us with her head draped over the other one's back. We found comfort in our togetherness.

One day I began to bleed from my girl-dog parts down below. I didn't understand what was going on and kept washing myself. Shortly after I had begun to bleed, Roxy did too. We still had to run, though, and some of the male dogs were showing an interest in us. My belly was sore, I didn't want to run, and I certainly didn't want the advances of the male dogs from the kennels.

Some days and nights later I found I wanted to try to get to the male dogs, but there was no way I could reach them as they were locked up, and so was I. I felt frustrated and tried to climb the walls, but I couldn't find my way out.

Being confined to those kennels could sometimes be terrifying because we couldn't escape from anything that scared us. One night the most frightening thing happened. It was when the weather had turned colder, and as usual Roxy and I were huddled together. We suddenly heard the loudest explosions coming from outside, and through the gap at the top of the kennel wall we could see bright lights every time we heard the crashing, banging thuds. We'd never encountered such noises before, and after each time the sounds roared, and the lights soared across the sky, we could hear excited human voices.

A strong smell filled the kennels making my mouth dry and my throat sore. We both wanted whatever was going on out there to stop. We curled up in the corner of our kennel, both shivering with fear, but no one came to check on us. Fear overwhelmed the kennels as we sensed the other dogs were just as terrified as we were.

And then, as suddenly as they had begun, the noises and bright lights stopped. The smell, though, it lingered for the rest of the night, along with a profound anxiety that whatever had happened might just happen again.

Chapter Three

On the Road

Time passed by slowly, and I think if I hadn't in the future seen how life *could* be, then I would have reluctantly accepted my lot; that I had this life which revolved around some weird world which seemed to depend on me running. All the time running, just running, and then time in the gloomy kennel block.

Greyhounds came and went from the kennels. Some I liked, some I could happily have done without ever meeting, but when Roxy was outside running and I wasn't, there were times when I was all alone, and I hated those times. On the whole, however, we greyhounds tend to get on well together, so most of the dogs I came across I got along with.

We greyhounds have a certain sleek, streamlined shape which makes us distinguishable from most other dogs. Because of the amount of time we spend with one another – away from humans, just greyhounds with our long bodies and very pointed, long faces – we become familiar with one another in a way that many other dogs perhaps don't. When racing, we only ever really meet other

25

greyhounds, so for a long time that's what we think all dogs look like.

Occasionally, however, we'd come across some of those collie dogs you see in the countryside. With their shorter snouts and black and white markings I think they look akin to a badger. Some people think those collies are the intellectual elite of the domesticated canine world. Well I think I have to say here that those humans have clearly never met a greyhound. I'd also like to point out that if they really think collie dogs are so intelligent, then why do those dogs waste their time chasing those woolly dogs who have the dreadlocks? It seems like such a waste of energy, and I don't think those woolly dogs are too impressed either.

Indeed, we sleek, long-dogs, we do seem to have a certain affinity with one another – and it was only in the years to come that I'd realize how much we depended on each other back then. Those times when Roxy wasn't in the kennel, I would often wonder whether she would perhaps not come back. She began to sometimes be away for a few days and nights at a time, then she'd return panting and exhausted, and smelling of things I didn't understand. Those scents, however, I would shortly come to recognize. They were the smells of a place that existed far, far away – so far that when I eventually went there I had to be taken on a long journey in the back of a vehicle.

The vehicle reeked of lots of different dogs. Some were dogs I knew well, and I could certainly smell Roxy, but many I was not familiar with. There was a stench of urine and muck and something else. *Blood?* I thought. Perhaps it was blood like I'd had when all the male dogs had shown an interest in me? Or perhaps it was blood like when I once caught my toe on a sharp stone when I was running around a field?

At the time it'd happened I'd squealed – and we greyhounds can squeal very loudly. I stopped still and held up my front left paw. One of the men came over and had a look at my foot. He sighed and shook his head, but then stroked me on the side of my neck. That rare demonstration of affection was nice and all that, but my foot was really sore. Once I was back in the dull kennel I delicately licked my toe pad, and made sure I kept it clean over the days that followed.

During those days of my confinement Roxy was taken out, but not me. I didn't get to go out at all, in fact, and had to limp outside to go to the toilet in the run. I didn't like doing that because it was dirty

– I liked to keep mine and Roxy's space clean. Anyway, the point I'm making here is that the blood I could smell in the vehicle could have been like that toe blood. Whatever it was, though, it made me feel uncomfortable and worried. I cowered into a corner and closed my eyes, only opening them when the vehicle stopped, and someone I knew from the kennels came and attached a rope to the big leather collar they'd put around my neck.

The first time that collar was put on me I'd been able to smell the scent of another dog from our kennels on it. When I was younger I sometimes used to hear that dog whining. I would sniff at her whenever I passed by her kennel, and sometimes we'd touch noses through the metal bars of her gate, but she always seemed to be so sad – perhaps her siblings had gone away too? Since the day the collar was put on me I'd not seen or heard her. She'd vanished, and it seemed as though wherever she'd gone she was no longer in need of the collar I'd been given.

Once we reached our destination on that day of my first long journey in the stinking vehicle, I could hear the other dogs before I could see them. When the door to the vehicle was opened, I warily jumped out and looked around me.

There were dogs just like me and Roxy everywhere. I had honestly never seen so many dogs in one place.

Chapter Four

Those Tasty, Greasy Sticks of Food

Every one of those dogs at the place I came to know as the track was similar to me. We have short, smooth fur, with a long body, and a long neck. We have a long, narrow, pointed face, and a very long, thin tail. There were none of those collie dogs there, or those woolly dogs such canines were prone to chasing. Each dog was standing with someone. Some were with smaller humans who I recognized as being a bit like puppies, only human ones. I came to like those little humans, mostly because whenever I saw them they were kind to me, but also because I came to learn they always smelled like they'd been eating tasty food.

Some dogs' leads were being held by ladies – I knew they were ladies because they smelled a bit like my sister and me, but not like my brothers and the men who took us to run around that field. It looked as though most of the dogs were with men; men who were not unlike the man who was holding onto the rope that was attached to my collar.

Most of the humans were eating food which was very different to the food that was put in my bowl on most days. Food wasn't put in my bowl on all days, however, and I never quite worked out why some days were food days and some days weren't. I felt my stomach contort with hunger pains and I realized that that particular day had been a non-food day. I heard it make a long, drawn out gurgling noise. The dogs around me heard – some of their bellies were making the same sounds. The humans didn't seem to have noticed. If they had, they certainly didn't give me anything to satisfy my hunger.

I noticed one big black and white dog – a male dog I was later to learn was named Max. He nuzzled against the boy who was holding him, and then gazed longingly at the paper wrapping in the boy's hand. The boy offered down a long, light brown, greasy, crispy piece of food. I could smell its luscious aroma from where I was standing; I longed for some of that food. As I watched Max devour the tasty morsel my stomach caved in, folding into itself and disintegrating into an empty, dehydrated bag of muscle.

Once they'd eaten their food, the humans led us all into a place where there were rows of cages. Some of the dogs had a basket muzzle put over their face. I was horrified – I hoped I wasn't going to have to wear one of those! Some of the dogs were forced into a large, narrow cage – one cage each. Then I heard the most horrific noise. It sounded like those noises which had banged and lit up the sky all those nights before, back when it had still been cold.

From where I was standing I had a clear view of what was happening. As soon as that noise sounded across the sky, a gate lifted at the front of each cage and the dogs came running out. It looked as though they were chasing one of those fluffy creatures with the long ears. All the people around me were suddenly shouting and screeching.

And I was terrified.

That night for the first time I slept in the back of the vehicle. A black male dog belonging to someone else was put in beside me. He turned his back to me and sighed. I put my head on my paws and sighed too. Neither of us could get comfortable because there wasn't really enough space for the two of us to stretch out. The humans were gone for a long time, and when they came back I was desperate to go to the toilet. They all seemed extraordinarily happy and a little wobbly on their feet. They were loud, and I could smell something on them I didn't recognize.

And food! I could definitely smell food on them!

The scents were coming from their clothes, their hands, and even their shoes. They were smells which were driving me crazy with hunger. I was certain it was just like the food the boy had given to that dog Max earlier on. As I deeply inhaled those scent molecules of mouth-watering food into my highly-sensitive nose, my stomach resumed its contortions. We were eventually allowed out to go to the toilet and were both given a few dry dog biscuits, but they weren't enough to satisfy the pains in my belly.

Once I'd eaten, the man took a sharp implement from his pocket and jabbed it into my back leg. It was sharp and sore. I wanted to squeal but I was too frightened to. That wasn't the first time that had happened, and I really wished they wouldn't do it. The man did the same to the other dog. He squealed. Our respective legs were rubbed, and then we were roughly bundled back into the vehicle. This time I lay with my head close to the male dog's face. He sniffed me, and we both sighed and went to sleep. I was glad I wasn't alone. I missed Roxy and longed for the comparatively carefree, cozy days long before; those days when she and I had been with our mother and siblings.

The following day that black dog and I were forced into those cage traps. Other dogs were already in the traps and some of them seemed excited, but I was absolutely petrified. Over my face someone had fitted one of those large muzzles. I didn't understand what was going on and tried to take in what was happening around me. In sheer panic I frantically tried to escape from the cage, but then I realized there was no way out. And then I heard that awful loud noise and the front of the trap opened up, offering me the escape route I'd been searching for.

And so I ran.

I was so scared, and I didn't know where I was running to, so I just followed the other dogs and ran for my life. As I neared the front of the pack of running dogs, I noticed the fluffy creature way out in front of us. It gave me something to focus on so I chased it. The black dog I'd spent the night with, so to speak, must have noticed it too. He was fast and he overtook all the other dogs. I wasn't too far behind him. And then, as quickly as it had all begun, the humans were waiting for us. The black dog was welcomed by his person and given a nice rub on his head and back. In the crowd I spotted the man who'd taken me there. He came over, stroked me on the head and told me 'Good girl!' So whatever had happened, it seemed that I'd done what he'd expected of me.

All I'd done had been to chase some other dogs and a fluffy creature around. I was very confused, but then I was handed one of those greasy, smelly food sticks I'd been coveting. I thought I'd died and gone to dog heaven. The man noticed my gazing eyes and gave me a couple more. Once he'd finished eating them he let me lick the paper. Lick the paper? I wanted to eat the paper! I was starving!

We ran several times that day, and each time it was a little easier and I became less frightened. My racing days had begun, and while I couldn't have known it then, that was how my life would be for some time.

Chapter Five

Rex

The first time I saw someone being cruel to a dog who had lost a race, I was horrified to the core of my dog soul – if dogs have a soul that is. I'm assured by Clare that if there really is a heaven, and if humans really do have souls, then surely dogs must have them too. It seems as though there are a lot of 'ifs' there, I thought Clare knew everything – clearly that isn't the case!

The dog was named Rex. A big, bold, strong dog he was and, boy, could he run? On the day in question, however, he took a stumble on the curve of the track and some other dogs overtook him. Some humans were roaring, some were screeching, some were jumping up and down with excitement. But poor old Rex bravely hobbled off the track to his handler. His handler grabbed him, attached a lead to his collar and pulled him away from the track.

From where I was standing with my own handler I could see what happened next. Poor Rex, who clearly had a very sore leg, was yanked by the lead into a corner away from the crowds of humans. The man punched him across the side of his face.

Rex squealed, and screamed and screamed. He cowered against the floor in fear at what was coming next. The man lifted his foot and kicked him on his side. Rex's body moved with the force of the kick and he curled into the corner. His whole body was quivering and he lay there whimpering. The man shook his head and spat at the ground beside Rex's head. The woman who was with him looked down at Rex and also shook her head.

A few other humans had seen what had happened and they shook their heads. I sensed they were upset about what they'd seen, but perhaps they were cross with Rex too. Whatever they were thinking, they didn't do anything about what they'd seen. All I wanted was for someone to go and rescue him, but no one did.

Deep inside me my fear intensified, and I glanced at the man who was holding onto my rope. I wondered whether he would ever do that to me. He looked back at me and shook his head – I wasn't sure what he meant, but he didn't seem angry with me. And then he stroked me on the head, and said 'Good girl.' We moved away to another part of the crowd. I felt reassured by his actions, and I think I knew from that point that he wouldn't do to me what that person had done to Rex.

Much later on, and as we were walking back to the vehicle, I saw Rex with the person who had hurt him. They were standing with another man, to whom Rex's handler gave some paper and then handed over Rex's lead. Rex hobbled away, hardly touching his sore front leg to the ground as he walked. I hoped the new man would be kinder to Rex, and that he would make his leg better. Just like my brothers, sisters and mother, however, I never saw Rex again.

The following day, once all the running was over and the sky had changed to being dark, we all sat in the vehicle and the humans ate those tasty, smelly sticks. My stomach ached once more for some of that food. Eventually me and the other dog, the black one I by then knew was named Lad, were each given one of those tasty sticks.

One.

I was very disappointed – I really could have eaten a whole dog bowl full of that delicious food.

Chapter Six

Just Another Day

That day on which I'd witnessed a particularly evil side of humans, a long journey in the vehicle led me back to the kennels, where Roxy was waiting for me. She smelt different – as though she, too, had been taken to one of those tracks on which dogs chase the fluffy creature. She seemed a little upset about something. I hoped no-one had hurt her like poor Rex had been hurt.

We greeted one another by gently wagging our tails in that understated way we greyhounds are prone to doing. It wasn't that we weren't pleased to see one another – just that we long dogs can sometimes be a little insular in our public demonstrations of affection.

Over the times that followed, our lives fell into some kind of routine. We were sometimes taken onto the big expanse of grass to chase one another, often staying out there for what felt like a whole day, at the end of which we were exhausted. On days that we didn't run in the field we were taken in a vehicle to a track, and then bundled into one of those cage traps so we could chase the fluffy creature. Sometimes I was there with Roxy, and other times I was there with others from the kennels, but always we ran, and occasionally we got some of that tasty human food. I worked out that whoever got around the track the fastest was the one who was given the most of those. This inspired me to run faster. I didn't care about that fluffy creature we had to chase, just about the tasty sticks of food.

There were times when days and nights would pass and we were not taken out at all. On those days we had to mess in our run, and we both hated doing that. At nights, Roxy and me, we would lie next to one another for comfort. I'd often lie with my head resting over her back, and sometimes she would rest hers over mine. She was the one thing that had been constant through all of the traumas of my short life. I missed her when she used to go off in the vehicle without me, and I got the impression that when I wasn't there she missed me too.

Just like my mother and other siblings had done, one day Roxy disappeared. I sensed something different about the way in which she was taken away. I couldn't put my paw on it, but it just felt, well, just different. I moped around for several days and nights and really thought I was never going to see her again, but then one day after those days and nights had passed, she was brought back to the kennels. Only this time she wasn't put back in beside me. I was alone, and she was alone in the kennel opposite. I could see her, but not rest my head across her back.

We whined across the corridor to one another. I was frustrated; she also seemed to be frustrated. I was scared; she seemed scared too. Sometimes we got to go out onto the grass together, and each time I hoped they would put us back together, but no, we were always put in separate pens. She smelt different – not as though she'd been running on the tracks, it was something else. Something I couldn't figure out.

The humans kept on coming in and looking at her. I tried to get their attention so they would remember the two of us were meant to be together. But it was to no avail; they weren't interested in me.

Some nights later our lives were propelled into an acknowledgement of adulthood; when we realized that things had changed forever. It was at a time when usually the only sounds would have been the gentle snores and occasional whimpering of the other dogs in their sleep, the soft scurrying of small rodents outside, and the urgent fluttering wings of those flying creatures of the night, that Roxy suddenly let out an excruciating cry.

She began to pant and her body curled into some strange convulsion. She looked through the bars of the kennel doors at me; reflected in her eyes I could see an image of the small shafts of moonlight which seeped through the cracks between the wood. Her eyes were open wide and shining with rims of whiteness at their edges, which told me she was frightened. I have to admit that I was scared too. I whined and hoped someone would come to help her soon.

She looked as though she was in the most awful pain, and those strange, contorted movements of her body continued, while her by then incessant panting stopped her from making any other sound. But then, after a while the strangest thing happened, and I watched in amazement as a slimy, black and white slug-like creature descended from between Roxy's hind legs.

I would have been petrified had that happened to me, but I saw her calmly reach over to the giant slug and start licking it. Lick, lick, lick, she went, methodically and vigorously. She did that for what seemed like ages, and then it looked as though she was tearing at it in an attempt to eat it. My stomach rumbled with hunger. I stood up and made an excited whimper to encourage her. Excitedly I licked my lips in anticipation of an impending feast. But then, quite suddenly, the shiny, slippery, slimy bag of black and white erupted and offered an urgent cry. It was a sound I'd heard many times from other parts of the kennel block.

It was a baby dog! Roxy had produced a baby greyhound.

Chapter Seven

Roxy's Litter

Through the rest of the night those tiny creatures kept on emerging from Roxy. One after another they tumbled their way into this world. Following her vigorous licking, eventually each one gasped and then called into the cold night air. I lay watching, wanting to help but feeling helpless.

As morning filtered in bands of bright light between those wooden panels which formed the walls of our kennels, the small, softly snuffling, yelping dogs used their tiny front paws to pull their way as close as they could get to Roxy. Eagerly they fed from her, and then nestled down next to her warm belly.

Every now and then, Roxy would stop panting and gently nuzzle those baby dogs, pushing them closer to her. She washed each of them in turn and nudged them with her nose, all the time tenderly snuggling her long body around them – carefully protecting them. I was worried she would crush them, they were so very fragile.

Dogs can't really count very high, however every dog seems to understand that one treat is the fewest amount of treats you can be given. More than that one treat you could perhaps describe as being a few, or even some, and when there are more than that you would perhaps describe the amount of those treats as being a lot, or even many. But if there was a great many of those treats, you'd probably call them an abundance, and your eyes would pop out of your head in excited anticipation! Well, if a great many treats is an abundance, then there was absolutely an abundance of those baby dogs wriggling their way around under Roxy's belly. Roxy looked weak and exhausted.

There was a smell lingering in the air of blood and other body fluids. It was so strong I found myself wanting to make a nest in the corner of my kennel, only there was nothing there for me to make a nest with, and no baby dogs for me to make a nest for.

The humans eventually arrived.

They marched straight into Roxy's kennel and lifted up the baby dogs they called puppies and turned each of them over and had a look at them. Once they had lifted each one and looked at their underneath, and opened each one's mouth to look inside, they put them back where they had found them. Roxy was distressed and stood up beside the humans, carefully watching what they were doing. As one by one they put each puppy back, Roxy followed the puppy with her nose, making sure it was safe, and then vigorously licking it and nudging it with her nose.

When they'd almost finished looking at all of the puppies, they picked up a small fawn one. The humans looked at one another and shook their heads. That one wasn't put back in Roxy's kennel. Instead it was put into a container. Roxy seemed alarmed that it hadn't been put with the others, and wasn't concentrating on the last few that were put back on the ground.

The humans left the kennels, taking the puppy in the container with them; meanwhile Roxy stood at the kennel gate, ignoring the puppies they had left behind. She stood at that gate for a long time and whined. When no one came back, her whines became soft, sad whimpering. Eventually she returned to the rest of the puppies. They were wriggling around and making soft whimpering sounds of their own, seemingly telling Roxy they needed to be fed.

Much later that day one of the humans returned and put some soft blanket bedding in with Roxy and the puppies. I'd have thought they would have brought back the missing puppy, but they didn't. Roxy must have thought so as well, because she was searching the bedding to see whether she could find it. Eventually she lay down and focused on the puppies they had left her with. With the one gone, there was still an abundance of them.

I desperately wanted to go and help Roxy to take care of them. I wanted to love them and pull them into my own belly, I wanted to lick them and help to toilet them, but all I could actually do was lie on my uncomfortable bed and watch between the bars of my kennel gate. I missed being able to lie with my head across Roxy's back.

After some days and nights the puppies were all taken away in a box. Roxy was inconsolable. She whined and whined, and then howled like our mother had done that time our siblings were taken. But then they brought them back, and she danced around them, waiting for each puppy to be put back in the bed. I could smell them from my kennel and they all smelled like whenever we cut ourselves. I was horrified that they would be bleeding – it looked as though the blood was coming from their tiny ears. Through the rest of that day Roxy washed each puppy from nose to tail, with each wash delicately soothing each puppy's sore ear.

As I watched those puppies grow into small dogs, my love for them grew and grew. I lay watching them and gave them names. There was Cheeky and Greedy and Pest and Cutie and Spotty and Stripy and Silly and White-leg and Patch and Little-Roxy. I even decided to give a name to the fawn one the humans had taken away. I named him Little One. We never saw him again – it often seemed as though our friendships and relationships with our fellow greyhounds were transient; just long dogs passing by one another in the grand scheme of greyhound goings-on.

I loved all those puppies, but most of all I loved Little-Roxy, mainly because she reminded me so much of Roxy. If I wanted one thing in those days and nights as I watched Roxy taking care of her puppies, it was for her to never be parted from them.

Chapter Eight

Puppy Love

Those puppies certainly kept Roxy busy. They were no longer quite so vulnerable, or in need of so much of her warmth and milk. In the absence of enough food being provided, however, even though her puppies had clearly begun to show an interest in solids, they also continued to want to feed from her. And so, ounce by ounce they drained every drop of milk they could possibly devour.

Her teats were huge, and those puppies with their emerging sharp puppy teeth dangled from her whenever they had the opportunity. With her being confined in such a small space with them she had no way of escaping their demands. She growled at them whenever they became too much for even her good nature. But they were so hungry; she, in turn, was exhausted, and her ribs were protruding.

The humans eventually seemed to realize that the puppies needed much more food, and a few times a day they came in with several bowls of dog kibble. Even though I didn't particularly like kibble, seeing it still made me hungry. I always ate mine as soon as it was brought to me. I felt ashamed with myself that I was drooling at the sight of that puppy kibble, but at least with all that food being provided for the puppies, Roxy was finally able to get a little rest.

Over the coming weeks I lay watching those puppies as they grew and grew. When I had to go running and I sensed I was close to returning to the kennel block, I became excited to see them. I loved to watch them as they played together, joyfully tumbling and gamboling over one another. They would sometimes play too rough, and one would offer a growl to tell the other puppy to back off – in doing so instinctively teaching each other the social skills they would need for dealing with other dogs they encountered in the future.

Roxy was weary, but I could tell she loved those puppies. She, too, seemed to have noticed the cheekiness and clinginess of Little-Roxy, and the two of them had developed a particularly strong bond. Little-Roxy followed her everywhere, and cried when Roxy was taken out to run in the field.

One day the humans came into the kennels, and instead of taking Roxy outside to run, they took the puppies – all of them. Roxy was beside herself and kept her eyes focused on the door to the big shed, all the time whining. From outside we could hear the playful barks and happy yips of the puppies.

Later... much later, the puppies were returned to Roxy. Roxy sniffed each of them in turn and licked their faces. Then she did it again, carefully sniffing at each one once more. I sensed there was something wrong with her, and she looked over at me with panic in her eyes. She looked at the door, back at the puppies, and then back at the door. All was quiet outside. She whimpered. And whined. And then she began to howl. I looked again at the puppies and realized that the abundance of young dogs had become only some. They were not all there – and Little-Roxy was one of those who had gone.

Roxy continued to howl, and then I joined in. The other dogs in the shed, the ones we couldn't see, they all began to howl too, mournfully adding to our chorus of despair. But no sound came from beyond the shed, and eventually we all lay down. Just as we'd always had to do, we accepted our lot and that we had no control over our lives. No choice. All that happened to us was in the hands of the people who made us run.

Roxy ushered her remaining puppies to lie down beside her. I knew what she was doing, we had experienced it before. She was cherishing any precious moments she had left with those puppies before they, too, were taken away from her – just as our siblings and mother had been taken away from us.

That day came only a few days and nights later. When the humans came in en masse, it was obvious to Roxy and me what they'd come for. Roxy tried her best to protect them; to prevent the humans from taking her puppies from her. In that non-aggressive and polite way we greyhounds have, she jumped around and whimpered, begging them to leave her remaining puppies behind. But it was all to no avail.

Once they'd removed the puppies, and Roxy had lain in soulful hopelessness, sometime later the humans returned to the shed and put Roxy back in beside me. It was bittersweet for both of us – we were back together, but she had loved those naughty puppies. And I had loved them from afar.

I lay beside her and she put her head across my back, just like the old days, but things were different. While we had the joy of our renewed companionship, I felt afraid. From the despondent, forlorn way Roxy seemed to be, I could tell that she was also afraid.

Chapter Nine

Running Days

Life returned to how it had been, with journeys that lasted too long, and multiple races against dogs I mostly didn't know, on tracks I had grown to despise.

Sometimes I'd come first and I would hear humans cheering and shouting. Strangely, even when I didn't win, I would still hear cheering and shouting, which didn't really make any sense to me. Perhaps it didn't actually really matter whether you won or not. Maybe it was simply taking part that mattered.

Life at the kennels became routine, but the temperature was sometimes too hot, and sometimes freezing. I hated both equally. When it was too hot, it was difficult to find somewhere cool to lie down because there was nowhere to go in order to escape from the heat. When it was too cold, Roxy and I huddled together on our uncomfortable beds and waited it out. Together we waited and hoped for the longer days to arrive when the weather would be warmer, and instead of freezing, icy snow and frost we would have warmness, and fresh rain would beat down against the glass panels near the ceiling on the far side of the shed.

I sometimes lay awake and watched that rain. I watched it forming small dots, and then as the rain got heavier it would run in channels of water down the window. When it rained like that and it was warm but cool at the same time, if we got out for a run we would see that the leaves had returned to the tall plants around the edges of the field.

And there were flying creatures, lots of those flying creatures chancing their luck at finding food amidst the long grass in the field. Each time they flew close to the ground, Roxy and me, we would race to chase them. We'd never catch them because they were far too fast for us, and they had that amazing way of soaring into the sky. I hesitate to add that they were probably far cleverer than we were. But then perhaps cleverness can be measured differently between animals who fly and animals who chase fluffy creatures around a track – we have different purposes in life, different needs, so who's to say who is the most intelligent?

Strangely, those were sometimes happy times, those afternoons running in the field with Roxy. I enjoyed running with the others in the field, too, it was so much nicer than the track. I much preferred to run free without the pressure of being forced to run and wear a muzzle around my face. But the best times were always with my sister Roxy.

All our exercise was in the field by then, and we no longer had to run on that machine – I don't know why they'd had us do that. Perhaps they were trying it out and had had second thoughts because they realized we didn't like it – that it was stressful. I don't think the man and the others were unkind, I think that they just didn't know that dogs could be treated better. I don't think they understood that there was a much nicer life possible for a greyhound. And I suppose that at that point neither did I know that. I wasn't to discover for some time that there was a world outside of running.

Chapter Ten

Max

The kennel opposite us, the one in which Roxy had given birth to her puppies, remained empty for some days and nights, many I think. Then one day a dog – a male dog – was put in there. I recognized him! He was Max, the large black and white dog I'd seen when I'd first been taken to the race track. He was the one who'd been with the young person who'd fed him all those juicy, tasty, greasy sticks of food.

He seemed to remember me too. He wagged his tail when he saw the two of us standing in the kennel opposite. He was a big, bold dog, but I could see he was nervous about being in that kennel for the first time. Roxy and me, we'd been there for our whole lives, and apart from our trips to go running, that dark, squalid kennel block was all we'd ever known.

Max kept on looking towards the door, just as Roxy had done when she'd had her puppies taken away. I wondered where Max's young person was, and imagined that was perhaps who he was looking for. Over the coming days and nights, even though Max got into the way of the kennels, he continued looking longingly over to the door. There were some days when the three of us were taken out to the field to run beside one another. Max was fast – he was a big, strong dog – but Roxy and me, we could hold our own, and every now and then we would outrun him.

Max liked to play, and often when we were being called back he'd race around the field again, coaxing us to follow him. He'd crouch down on his front paws and then stand up and dance around us. If we ever gave in to his invitation to play by chasing him, he'd turn around and chase us back the way we'd come – I'd never met a dog who was quite as much fun as he was. Sometimes he'd get to be too much, though, and I would turn and nip at him, but he simply thought I was encouraging him... and he would chase me all the more.

He occasionally went away with Roxy to race at the tracks and I was left alone – I could smell the scents of the track on them when they returned. Other times Roxy and I would go together, and sometimes I went with Max, and Roxy was left behind. All the time while we were waiting to run Max would look as though he was searching the faces of the humans who were there. I was sure he was on the lookout for that young person who'd fed him the tasty food.

On a few occasions during the time when Roxy was having her lady time (which all we female dogs seemed to have from time to time, although I'd noticed mine seemed to have stopped altogether), she was taken out with Max quite a lot and I was left on my own. One time they were gone for a few hours and then the two of them returned. Around that time Max would spend all day whining and wanting to come over to our kennel, he was so frustrated. When Roxy finished her lady time he settled down again.

Shortly after their absence from the kennel block Roxy stopped going off to the track again, and instead it was Max and me who went to race. One time after a long journey we ended up at the track at which I'd first met him – he seemed to recognize the track too. He became extremely excited; all the time he was scanning the faces of the humans there, desperately looking for his person.

After his race, which of course he won, and mine in which I'd been pipped at the post by two dogs: a large stripy dog and a big dark grey monster of a dog, suddenly a young person came running over to Max and me.

Max was beside himself with joy – it really was *his* person. His young person. My handler gave Max's rope over to the young person, and the young person and Max danced around one another with excitement. It was quite embarrassing actually, as we greyhounds are normally much more reserved than that and, as I've said, we don't tend to give in to being overenthusiastic about things.

In the end, that was the last time I ever saw Max. His tail was joyfully wagging as he walked away, happily trotting along beside his person. Every now and then the person reached across to stroke Max's long, black and white head. When they reached the other side of the crowd, Max turned and looked in my direction one last time.

I think if he'd been human he would have given me a thumbs up.

Chapter Eleven

Little-Max and the Others

Sometime after Max had walked out of our lives, happy, I was sure, to be back with his person, the humans came and split Roxy and me up again. She was put back in the kennel opposite and I noticed she'd become extremely large around her belly. We both whined across the corridor because we were desperate to be together, but no matter how much we howled and called to one another, no one came to move us. So, instead, we watched each other from across the corridor. She continued to put on weight and she smelt differently – just like she had that time before when those puppies had come squeezing out of her.

Right enough, over the coming days and nights she became restless. This time the humans had given her some extra blankets in which to make a nest. She desperately turned around and around in those blankets trying to get comfortable. And then, one evening as the light was disappearing from the sky, more puppies began to emerge from her. In the time between each of the puppies emerging, she licked and licked the previous one, and then pushed hard to get the next one to come out. It looked extremely sore, and eventually there was once again an abundance of those little dogs around her... all whimpering and demanding her maternal love.

When, as before, the humans came and looked at all the puppies, that time they left them all with Roxy. Once they'd gone she carefully continued to wash each puppy in turn. It looked as though she might just have been counting them, although I was sure she wasn't actually able to count. I longed to go and take a few of those little dogs and look after them for her. I think there was something quite selfish in how I felt, because every part of my body was aching to be able to have my own puppies.

For the puppies, everything after that happened pretty much as it had with the previous ones: the ear marking causing their tiny puppy ears to bleed; their interest in food once they'd stopped suckling so much; I even gave them all names again. In that litter there was a large puppy who looked just like Max, and I named him Little-Max. He was bold and cheeky and always first to get his food.

And then, one day they were all gone and Roxy was put back in beside me. After pining for what felt like days on end, and my trying to console her by staying close to her, Roxy and I fell back into our old routine.

Meanwhile, every now and then I was taken out and given more injections into my back leg. Those injections were sore and I was never really sure why I was being given them. Running had become my forte. And run I did. I think that was my thing – I had become very fast. And I think because of that I was taken out a lot to run, sometimes in the field with Roxy and the others, but also to the tracks. I hated being away from the others, but I got a lot of attention when I ran well.

Chapter Twelve

Disappearing Dogs and the Ways of the Track

Sometimes at the track I used to see other dogs who were being held tightly, and I would watch as a human pushed a very sharp object into their leg – in the same way they sometimes did to me. I'd noticed my lady time had stopped altogether.

Clare explains that this was probably because of the injection, and because I was mostly used for running, whereas dogs like Roxy were used for running *and* breeding. As I was mostly on the track it was used as a way of stopping the male dogs from paying me too much attention. Shortly after each injection I used to feel quite anxious and stressed, angry almost, which was a strange feeling for someone as friendly as I am. Clare says that it, too, can be a side effect of some of those injections.

There were other troubling things that I saw on those days at the tracks, things which bothered me quite a lot. The dog named Lad I sometimes shared the vehicle with in those early days, there was one time I saw him getting ready to go running in a race and I noticed his handler was avidly chewing on something he'd removed from a small packet. Shortly before Lad was due to run, the man pulled the thing he was chewing from his mouth, lifted up Lad's foot and put some of the sticky chewy stuff between his toes. Well, needless to say, when the race began and the gates were lifted, Lad couldn't run so well that day. At the end of the race, even though Lad hobbled in to the finish line last, I noticed his handler didn't seem to be upset. In fact, he seemed delighted, and promptly enthusiastically rewarded Lad with a handful of tasty food.

Now I know for a fact that Lad would normally have had a chance of beating all the dogs in that race. The only dog who would have come close would have been Nero, and Nero was the one who won. I suppose that was always going to happen without him having Lad a short way in front of him. When the humans came to remove the sticky stuff from between Lad's toes, he was incredibly stressed about it, because whatever it was had stuck to his pads and the hairs between them.

I saw many dogs being hit by their handler when they didn't do well in a race. I was never hit, and I don't think Roxy or the others were, but I wasn't always with them so I don't know for sure. Max was certainly never mistreated in that way. After all, Max had a person who gave him those tasty sticks to eat, and who seemed to care about him. But during those days and nights when he was in our cold kennel building, even Max had been forced to spend that time away from someone he clearly loved. I think he was lucky to have been able to have gone back to his young person. But some humans were actually quite horrible, and I lived in fear of those sorts of humans.

The cases of the disappearing dogs used to bother me – I was curious to know why they were no longer around. But I suppose with dogs being dogs and us having the difficulty of not being able to fully communicate with humans, I'll never find out what happened to them. It's just so strange that they would disappear like that – and so many of them.

Dogs would often disappear after they'd had some kind of accident on the track. Or sometimes they would disappear after they'd given birth to many of those baby greyhounds. Even some of those baby greyhounds disappeared never to be seen again, but there seemed to be no rhyme or reason to when and how the disappearing happened.

The racing injuries I saw in some dogs looked

terribly painful, and some of them would writhe in agony after having tripped or fallen on the track. Many dogs would come back from the race holding up a leg, some of them hobbling along with more than one sore leg. Some dogs' legs were floppy as they walked, and some would hold them at odd angles.

The worst times of all, though, were those times when, once they'd been hurt, the dogs couldn't stand up. They lay there on the ground where they had fallen, and often they squealed with all the pain they were in. Some dogs' injuries were so bad their body had become numb and their legs were extended out straight. With others, when someone tried to lift a paw or their tail, it was floppy – as though they couldn't feel a thing. I saw some dogs who couldn't stand up at all, and some who couldn't even lift their head.

Help would often be a long time in coming, but then eventually someone would come and lift the dog away. Sometimes, but not so often, someone would come with one of those sharp objects and stab the dog in the front leg with it – and then very quickly the dog would go quiet and stop breathing. I remember a collapsed dog once being removed from the track after he'd had an accident, and then

I heard a loud bang in the distance and his painful cries immediately stopped. I wasn't really sure what had happened – only that the noise had terrified me.

After seeing all that I'd seen on the track, I hoped that I would never be one of those dogs who hurt themselves.

Alas, my time would come sooner than I'd expected.

Chapter Thirteen

No Going Back

I'm old now and it's difficult to recall exactly what happened on the day I was injured. I assume it's the same with humans, in that we have a way of blocking out a traumatic experience, and then your memories really do become a blur as time speeds forwards (Clare concurs that it is the same for humans). The times you had back then, well they do become more difficult to remember. There *are* aspects from the 'day of the accident' I do recall, but I truly think some of the details I've blocked out because it's simply too upsetting for me to think about that time in my life.

I know there was a very sharp bend on the track on which it happened, and I'm sure there was another dog quite close to me – a stripy dog if I remember rightly. I was determined I was going to catch up with that fluffy creature first, but then suddenly I felt some deep, excruciating feeling deep in the muscle of my front left leg. At the same time my back right leg twisted. And I stopped, right there in the middle of the track, and all the other dogs raced past me. I then let out a piercing greyhound scream of pain.

I was sore, so very sore. I can recall wondering what I should do. Should I turn and go back the way I had come? Or should I head to the fluffy creature anyway – even though I had no chance of getting there first? I decided to go towards the creature, because if I headed back I would only be closer to those traps, and that awful starting sound I hated so much.

I dotted my foot to the ground, but then I realized I was simply going to have to walk on three legs. Three legs? I had never walked on three legs before in my life – even that time I cut my toe I was still able to put my foot to the ground every now and then.

I was in agony!

My handler was quite good about it really – especially when I think of the horror I'd seen when so many of the other dogs had got hurt while running. He had a quick look at my sore legs, and then after waiting around for a while at the track (which I thought was quite unreasonable given the circumstances) we eventually got in the vehicle. He lifted me in as there was no way I was able to jump in.

After a long journey home I was put back in with

Roxy. We were so very happy to see one another, but I was unable to express just how happy I was because of being in so much pain. She let me rest my head over her back and she occasionally licked my sore legs. She knew, somehow she knew.

Over the next few days I was taken into the field, I think to see whether I could run. How much more could I do to tell them that my legs were blooming painful? In the end they bundled me into a vehicle and I was taken to a place where there were many frightened animals. Someone there held my sore front leg and poked at it, and then they went on to manipulate and poke at the other sore back leg. For the sake of completion, I think, they also manipulated the two good legs, but that just made me have to put weight on my sore ones.

I told them quite forcefully with a squeal whenever what they did was painful. Finally, the man just nodded his head and stood up to speak to my handler. He was shaking his head by then, and I thought to myself, *uh oh, this doesn't look so good!* Perhaps this was the place where some of those other dogs had disappeared to? That shaking of the head thing, well in my experience with observing other dogs and their handlers, it had never been a good sign.

The man who'd examined me handed over a bottle of something and sent us on our way. That was when I first discovered the art of spitting out tablets. It came quite naturally, so in the end they put it in my food, which I ate quite willingly. That had been quite a result... and I've remembered that trick to this day.

Over the coming days, and despite the tablets I was having, my leg didn't mend. After being taken out to run around the field a few times, I realized that perhaps I would never run again. Each time I placed my foot on the floor it felt as though my whole leg was hot and painful – especially at the top near my elbow and shoulder. At the same time, my back leg throbbed whenever I moved from sitting to standing, or vice versa. It was no good – and the humans also seemed to know I wasn't getting much better. More importantly to their minds, I suppose, it looked as though I wasn't going to be able to run any more.

In the field one day after they'd been encouraging me to run with Roxy and the others, the people put all the other dogs back into the kennels. They then stood around me shaking their heads. I really didn't like that shaking head thing! And then, as I came limping over to them, one of them patted me on the head and said something. There was a stranger with them, and without any warning this new person put me on a rope and led me away from the rest of the humans.

Something felt different. Where was I going? Not to the track, that was for sure – there was no way I'd have been able to have run. The person opened a vehicle door, and as I was lifted into the back of it, I suddenly remembered Roxy. I panicked! I tried to leap back out of the car, but the human forced me to stay. What could I do? I was powerless – I had no choice but to go with her. Reluctantly, I settled down on the soft dog bed in the back of the vehicle. I could smell dogs, many different dogs.

I sighed.

Roxy had been left behind all alone in the kennel, and I was going somewhere else with someone I'd never seen before. My mind drifted to all the greyhounds who we'd shared the kennels with, all the dogs I'd ever encountered, and then I realized – perhaps that time I was going to be the one who didn't go back.

I worried that I might never see Roxy again. A sick, frightened, sad feeling started in my chest and filled my body.

Part Two

A Place to Call Home

A Dog Like Peggy

Chapter One

The V-E-T and the Mixed Hierarchy of Greyhounds

At first it felt as though I'd simply been shifted from one racing kennels to another... only I quickly realized this new kennels was different. In this one I was given a big bed with lots of soft bedding in which to snuggle down – it was even better than the extra bedding Roxy had eventually been given when she had her puppies. I was given heaps of yummy food, and the lady who took care of us was very kind to us. She gave us a lot of fuss and regularly came to check we were okay.

We were taken out for walks along country lanes each day, and we sometimes went to play in the nearby field. At first I didn't want to play so much because of my sore legs, but over time it became much easier to get around.

There were other dogs like me there, not as many I think as Roxy had given birth to that first time when she had an abundance of baby dogs, but there was definitely more than a few of us. I shared a kennel with another dog – Helga.

Helga was one of those greyhounds who was very unsure of herself. I got the impression she was a little older than I was, and that she'd perhaps not been treated so well when she'd been on the tracks. Whenever we went out for walks, she was extremely nervous about the vehicles which passed us along the road. She was also scared of having her rope attached to her collar to go out. Because of that, whenever she heard the people coming over to the kennels to take us for our exercise, she'd start quivering with fear. I was sure those people would never hurt us, with Helga, though, it seemed as though she didn't trust a single person in the world.

Just after arriving at the kennels I was taken to one of those very frightening places where there were people who reeked of other dogs, and where I could smell other creatures quite unlike dogs. It was just like the place I'd eventually visited in the days after I'd hurt my leg on the track.

In that place there was a person who was apparently known as THE VET. She poked around at all of my legs, but just like on the previous occasion, particularly the sore ones, which I felt was a little mean. I thought that was going to be the end of it, but then a few days later I was back there, amid the many other very stressed and poorly dogs.

And then I spotted them, the source of that strange scent I'd been puzzled about the time before. They were small creatures with tiny, pointed ears. They all did a weird thing whereby they opened their mouth wide and let out piercing screams. Whenever I got anywhere close to them they pulled back their cheeks and made loud hissing sounds. I immediately decided I didn't like those spitting, snarling, spiteful, malicious creatures – they were quite nasty. Yes, horrible little attention-seeking creatures was the first impression I had of them. Much as I tried to ignore them, I found myself wondering what it might be like to chase one.

Chasing was definitely off the agenda for me on that day, because the nice lady who'd been looking after me since the racing days handed me over to someone else who smelled of many creatures. I turned and sadly watched my nice lady walk away from us. At the door she looked back and said something, but I didn't understand human speak. I only knew that she didn't sound angry with me. I guessed the only option I had was to follow the person who smelled of other creatures. She took me through to a room where there were animals locked up in cages which were much smaller than my kennel. Those creatures all seemed very anxious. I hoped I wasn't going to have to go into one of those cages.

Hoping wasn't enough to prevent the inevitable, and I was taken over to one of the larger empty cages. The lady opened the door. She told me to go inside and, again, I did as I was told. I was so very frightened, and I could sense a similar fear on all the creatures around me. I was sure they could sense that I was scared too. I began to shake uncontrollably.

Someone eventually came to fetch me and I was taken through to another room. I recognized the VET from our previous encounter a few days and nights earlier. She stroked me on the head and I realized I quite liked her – and then she stabbed me in the back leg with something sharp. I wasn't sure I liked her so much after all! They put me on a soft bed on the floor and one of them sat next to me, carefully stroking my neck. While I was pondering over whether or not I actually liked those people, I began to feel drowsy.

I don't recall what happened after that, until I gradually became aware once more of what was going on around me. I felt drowsy and was in a lot of pain. Only the discomfort wasn't just coming from my sore leg – that was certainly sore and felt as though someone had been tugging at it, but no, the hurt was coming from deep inside my belly.

Much later on I could see through the window that night time had arrived. Some of the animals in the cages beside me left, and each of them had seemed to be very uncomfortable in some way when they were taken from the cages. Eventually only a few of us remained, and we all seemed to be seeking respite from our respective throbbing, aching parts, not understanding why we were there and why we hurt so much. One dog was crying a lot, and some people came in to visit him. He wagged his tail a little when they arrived. They stayed a while and then went away again. He seemed terribly sad.

Much later on I was taken outside to do my business, and it was sore to crouch but I somehow managed. A huge sense of relief flooded through my body as I created a large puddle on the ground. When we went back inside I was put into a bigger kennel and given a little food and a bowl of water. Even after all I'd been through I was not going to refuse food. So I ate it all up, and then one of the people who smelled of lots of different animals came and sat down beside me in the kennel. She stroked my head and neck and checked my belly where I felt sore. Her voice was soothing and I drifted to sleep with my head across her lap.

I was suddenly awoken by the sound of a loud bell ringing. The nice person grabbed an object that was next to her and put it to her ear. She began to speak. She then shuffled out from underneath my head and stood up. She continued talking into the object, and even in my semiconscious, disconnected state, I realized there was something wrong.

She walked out of the kennel room, and suddenly a bright light flooded through the glass in the door. Shortly after this, more people arrived, and I could hear them all rushing around and making strange noises. The person who'd stabbed me before I'd gone to sleep was there, and I hoped they were all going to leave me alone – I'd already been through so much earlier on that day.

But no, it seemed that whatever they were doing, it wasn't going to be to me. As I lay there pondering, there was suddenly an almighty racket as one of those pointy-eared creatures was brought into the other room. I could hear it – it was wailing at the top of its voice. It was clearly demanding some immediate attention. I had never heard anything quite like it. I could hear people talking, and still the creature wailed. Now, I know I'd already decided I wasn't that keen on those creatures, but it sounded as though that one needed help!

And then, everything became quiet.

Somehow I managed to nod off to sleep again. I lay there soundly sleeping, blissfully unaware of what was going on in the room next door. In my slumber I returned to those days of running on the tracks. I could sense that Roxy was near me and we were in our kennel together, then I was back on the track and reliving the time when I hurt my leg. It's strange how we dogs can do that. You could be in a situation and know you're not on a track, but then you drift to sleep and you find yourself on the track again. But then something wakes you and you are back where you were before you went to sleep... and the other dogs from days gone by have suddenly disappeared...

And so, there I was running behind some other dogs and trying to catch up with them, but I couldn't quite reach them (which was a bit of a recurring nightmare for me), when something jolted me back to reality. Soft cries and whimpering grunts were emanating from one of the cages on the other side of the room. For a few moments I thought I was back with Roxy and her baby dogs, but realized very quickly that wasn't the case. A dull, hollow feeling of sadness filled my body. I felt it deep inside my chest and ached so much to be with Roxy again.

The sounds were coming from that creature, the one with the pointed ears who'd previously been wailing. I could see there were lots of giant slugs (I was sure they weren't puppies) crawling all over her! They were making whimpering sounds just like Roxy's puppies had done. That pointy-eared creature must have been giving birth to slugs when she arrived. She really had been making something of a meal of it with all her loud calling, however a little sympathy for her washed over me as I recalled how sore giving birth had been for Roxy!

Clare says it sounds as though the creature had had a thing known as a caesarean, whereby the baby creatures are cut out of the belly! Goodness me, I don't know which is worse, cutting them out or having them the way that Roxy had them! Clare adds that it's also likely those slugs were kittens, not slugs... but I'm not convinced!

Once she'd finished looking after the creature with

the pointed ears, the nice person checked on me several times until all the lights went out once more. I lay on my side and waited for daylight to come. My belly hurt so much, and I wondered whether the pointy-eared creature's belly hurt too. I felt sad that on that day no one had come to take me back to Helga and my other friends at the kennels. I lay thinking about whether I would ever see them again. But then the calming, soft, muffled sounds of the kittens eventually helped me to drift off to sleep.

Morning arrived, and again the people seemed to be really busy. The nice person came to take me outside again so I could create another puddle. Shortly afterwards I was taken through to another room. I walked very delicately because I was actually still very sore. And then I spotted the lady who'd been taking care of me since I left the racing kennels. I carefully wagged my tail. She came over and gently stroked my head and neck, and then she reached down and hugged me close to her. That hadn't happened very often in my life until I met her, but I realized I loved it when people did that.

Getting into her vehicle outside was difficult, but there was no way I was staying in the place where the VET lived. I did have to go back there again some days and nights later, but after standing quivering with fear in the place where all the animals waited, I was taken through to see someone. I was only in there for a short time – there were a few tugs on the skin of my tummy, and then we left for our journey to return to Helga and the others. Safely back in the vehicle, I sighed. I was grateful that my traumatic ordeal appeared to be over!

Life fell into a routine, and I quite liked my life then. I suppose that I didn't really know at that point that it could become even better. Apparently there exists some sort of lifestyle hierarchy for a greyhound. This greyhound hierarchy goes something like this:

The worst type of life is being a greyhound who has a nasty handler who doesn't care about greyhounds. They only have greyhounds to see how much money they can make from them, and once they have finished with them they do away with them – by whatever means. They also treat their greyhounds very badly, punishing them when they don't win. I'm glad I wasn't one of those greyhounds. Some of those dogs are even taken to other countries on a huge machine in the sky; in those other countries the dogs are often treated even worse than in my country – and that's saying something!

The next type of situation some greyhounds are born into is being a greyhound who has a handler who quite likes greyhounds but doesn't want to keep them once they can't run any more. Once their running days are over and they're no longer any use, they find somewhere for them to go so they can live somewhere else. I suppose that's the category which applies to me; I had been useful – and then I wasn't.

It seems as though some people who race greyhounds do actually keep them once they've finished their running days, which is quite nice and everything, but really greyhounds are quite lazy dogs and would prefer not to have been racing in the first place. On a very basic level, imagine getting up one day and feeling that your tummy's a bit sore, or perhaps you've got a bit of a headache, well that's how greyhounds sometimes feel as well and, quite frankly, there are occasions when we'd rather not have to go and run with a hungry tummy after having spent ages in a vehicle.

It's all about choice really, in the grand scheme of things. I predict that if you were to ask any greyhound what they would prefer to do with their life: live in a kennel and be a running dog on those awful tracks; live in a kennel and have to breed and breed until your body goes thin like Roxy had to; or live in a home with people who care about you, and who feed you nice food and take you out to see nice places, I would shake paws with you and bet you any amount of dog treats in the world all greyhounds would choose the latter.

So, if a dog is very lucky, the next stage in the hierarchy is to be taken to a rescue kennel. This is sometimes followed by a foster home. But the very lucky dogs go straight into the dog utopia for ex-racing greyhounds, the much-coveted (when you know they exist anyway) forever home.

So, knowing what I know now, and having experienced the life of a greyhound (me being a greyhound I suppose that's all I can experience, because it's quite obvious I'm not a Dalmatian or whatever, but you get the point I'm making), the best thing for any of us, or any dog for that matter, is to find one of those lovely forever homes.

For me, though, I was to wait a while longer before I was to find my own home I could have forever – with Clare and her family. I'll come to that later, because first of all I was to experience that sometimes intermediate stage: the foster home!

**Just me – on one of those comfortable sofas I
eventually discovered**

Chapter Two

Foster Dog

I was sad to be leaving the nice lady and the other greyhounds, but some other nice people were the next pit stop on my journey towards finding my utopia of a forever home.

The foster home was to be my first experience of being a part of what is known as A FAMILY. It was also to be my first experience of a number of other things. What follows here is a very personal list of things I very quickly realized I liked about being a part of a family:

Not being in a cage – all my life I had been in kennels or in a cage and I was finally free to go about the place as much as I wanted. I was free to roam around and go and put my head on people's laps, I was free to move from room to room, or let people know I wanted to go into the garden to spend a penny. I had hated being confined to a cage – why would anyone do that to a dog?

Children – children always smell of lovely food and are always really kind to me. They hug me and make me feel happy.

Food – not *just* food, because I'd always had food of sorts, but there had been times when the gaps between meals was particularly long. In a home I realized there was food I could go and access whenever I liked and, even better, food that was sometimes given to me by those aforementioned children.

Children are easy sources of what are known as treats. All a dog has to do is look longingly at the place where the treats are kept, or gaze lovingly at whatever the child is eating, and there you have it – the hand comes out and the child (or adult sometimes, but adults are not such easy prey) offers the nice food. What I will say, though, is that it's hardly ever any of those tasty, greasy sticks like the people ate at the race track!

Oops, Clare's interjecting here, because it seems she's a bit fed up of me going on about those tasty sticks of food, which, she now informs me, are known as chips. If you're in the UK anyway, elsewhere people call them fries. She tells me they're not good for greyhounds. She's such a spoilsport. She says that they're not good for other dogs either, and they're apparently not even good for humans. In that case, I think humans should get their act together and stop tempting me!

Living in a house – a house contains everything a dog needs and protects us from the weather. When it's too hot we have the chance to go and find somewhere cool to lie down, and when it's too cold there's a thing called central heating and somewhere to snuggle, be it a cozy dog bed or a sofa. In a kennel the confinement makes it impossible to get away from draughts or hotspots, because you're just stuck in that one miserable, restricted place.

Although sofas are clearly a part of living in a house, they deserve a mention all of their own:

Sofas – when I discovered sofas I thought I had ascended to a canine utopia. If you have a sofa to lie on just for yourself, it is the most comfortable thing in the world. It's unfortunate that other dogs, and humans of course, seem to think so too!

Regular Walks – this was a strange one because throughout my life there had always been exercise of sorts, but when you're part of a family, you get to know a routine, of which walks appear to be a part. It felt nice to know when to expect to have my rope put on so I could go for a walk. We dogs like routine.

Other dogs – I'd always been with other dogs, and

there wasn't a day that went by when I didn't miss Roxy and wonder how she was doing, but luckily the foster home had two other dogs. Those two greyhounds seemed to sense that I needed a bit of support, so right from the start they were very nice to me. They even sometimes allowed me to share their cozy beds, even though I'd been given one of my own.

Toys – we had toys in the rescue kennels, but at the foster home there was an abundance of toys, and I carefully carried them around in my mouth – a bit like Roxy used to with those puppies of hers. What was great was that the other dogs in the foster house were quite happy to share their toys with me. Honestly, those two dogs were typical of us greyhounds, we're the laid-back hippies of the dog world!

I thought at the time that the life I had there was how it was going to be for me forever. I fitted in with them all really quickly and had become really fond of them, but what I didn't know then was that the final move for me was going to be to find my own family. I hadn't known that the fosterers weren't going to be *my* family. Clare tells me that actually the people HAD considered keeping me because I'd fitted in so well, but she and her family had come along and wanted to love me instead. This was good because that meant that a space was created with the fosterers for another greyhound to have the chance to find out what it was like to be part of a family.

And so, having spent all that time in the rescue kennels, and having finally made my way to the foster home, it really wasn't that long before I was chosen by Clare and her family to be their forever dog. A forever dog is one who is going to be with that person forever, it's sort of just what it sounds like it would be, but I just like saying it. Forever dog... forever dog... forever dog... forever dog... Anyway, you get what I mean.

So, on with the story and how Clare and the others found me.

Chapter Three

Forever Dog

Clare and the others had been through a traumatic time during which their three old dogs had all passed away in a short space of time. This had created room in their hearts for more dogs, and their search first led them to Ralph, and after some days and nights, to me.

It seems there'd been a picture of me featured on the World Wide Web rescue page run by the charity who was looking after me. Clare and the rest of the family had seen it, and they'd felt sorry for me because the picture had ended up making me look not quite as attractive as my rescuers had intended. Clare saw my picture and thought I would never find anyone to love me, and that they should save me from a life without a forever home. It's not that I'm not attractive; it's just that I'm not that photogenic. They say the camera never lies, well in my case I think it did, but then I suppose that in the end that worked to my advantage.

They felt incredibly bad when they met me for the first time and they saw that I was actually quite pretty. I'm so glad they didn't just leave me there because I wasn't ugly enough, because in the end it wasn't so much that they were rescuing me, it seemed I was rescuing them. It appeared I was also rescuing that lump of a dog, Ralph, who they brought along to meet me at my foster home.

Oh yes: Ralph, Ralphie, Ralphie-Poos, Ralph My Love, Ralphie-Handsome, Handsome Boy, Ralphus ralphus, which is apparently his Latin name. Oh yes, we all know about Ralph. Then I didn't, of course, because on that day when I first met him all I could see was this dog with large ears who had the look of a greyhound, but who wasn't really one. He was a fake, a fraud, an imposter! In the years that followed I became aware that people would sometimes assume he was a greyhound, or they'd group him together with me when talking about our family. They would say things like, 'You know, the people with the greyhounds.' Well, I want to say, right here, and right now, that he isn't one! Not that I'm being breed-ist or anything, it's just that I like people to get their facts straight.

Ralph is taller than I am, but not as sleek somehow. His back is shorter than mine – I'm lower to the ground and have a longer back and a longer tail – this is so I can run like the wind. He can certainly run fast and would outpace most dogs, but on a greyhound scale, he is really not quick at all.

His face is broader than mine, it's still quite pointed, but his muzzle is more like a dog that looks a bit like one of us, but is longer haired and has fluffy ears – a Suzuki or something like that. Clare has just told me they're called salukis, not Suzukis! Anyway, sometimes he looks like one of those. His coat is sort of sandy like some of those dogs have, too, but he just doesn't have the long fur.

I liked my foster family, and as I said they may have kept me if Ralph and his people hadn't come along. The foster family was very nice and very kind to me, but I decided I liked this other family too, so in hindsight I imagine I was lucky to have had two potential forever homes coming along about that time. Indeed, I was a lot luckier than some of the other dogs from those running days – and many other shelter dogs who don't *ever* get the offer of a single home to live in forever.

I don't think Ralph was ever used for running. I think it would have been a great mistake if he had been! No, I think he was used for something else, and wherever he was, and whatever he was doing, I don't think he was treated very well. When I met him I was reminded of the greyhounds I would sometimes see cruelly treated by their handlers when they didn't win the races; the dogs who strangely disappeared – like that poor greyhound Rex.

So I immediately sensed that Ralph had deep-rooted psychological problems, and I like to think that over the years I have helped him with those – I think he sees from me that some things are just not worth being scared of.

Ralph is frightened of most people and seems to think everyone he meets represents some kind of threat to him. He also yawns a lot, which is apparently a sign to tell another individual that he is no threat to them. This is usually another dog, but some of us also tend to use it with people, or even objects in Ralph's case, which is just a little bizarre. Anyway, no threat to them? Ralph would never hurt a fly!

Clare tells me it's a lot more complicated than that, and that it's all about how we dogs interact with one another, and how we also sometimes try this special signaling language of ours as part of our dog-human communication repertoire. She says it sometimes gets lost in translation, resulting in a lot of people not necessarily picking up on what we're trying to say with our subtle expressions and postures. Because of Ralph's anxiety, he just uses the yawning thing a lot more than most other dogs do.

I can certainly reassure Ralph that I know from all my experience in this world that once you're in a home with nice, soft sofas, and regular food and cuddles, well, it's highly likely that the people who are giving you all that stuff, they tend to be nice people. He's getting there, but it's taken him a long time to truly trust people. I've actually noticed he certainly yawns less often now than he used to, which must be a good sign. Those people we live with, though, I could tell straight away they were a soft touch, but Ralph, well, Ralph needed time to recover from whatever suffering he'd been through before.

I'm not saying I was entirely brave, as there were still things I had to overcome, such as stairs for instance! Whoever invented stairs did not consider that at some point in the future we canines would be sharing human homes, and stairs and we long dogs take a little maneuvering. There are usually two steps between the step that our back feet are on and the step that our front feet are on, and when you're running up the stairs to get bedtime treats, or down in the morning to go out to create a puddle (and get more treats of course), then it is easy for us to get our legs in a tangle. Those steps were certainly not designed for greyhounds.

Ralph had clearly already encountered stairs by the time I came on the scene, and he took great pleasure in demonstrating his prowess at ascending them and then coming back down. That was when I first noticed his playful side. He raced up the steps and looked back at me wagging his tail, but at the same time he was encouraging me as I struggled to know where to put my darned feet! When I got to the top, mentally exhausted, he danced around me in excitement. It was just as though he was congratulating me for my physical achievement.

He showed me the way to one of the rooms where there were human beds, dog beds, and a heap of toys. He picked up one of the toys and his front end went down as he chewed it and it squeaked. Once he'd finished chewing at it, he flung it high in the air so it landed right next to me. When I went to grab it, he came over and snatched it from me and raced down the steps with it. 'Boy, he's going to be trouble!' I thought to myself, as I gingerly negotiated my way back down the steep stairs in pursuit of the stolen toy.

Really Ralph?

Chapter Four

The Importance of Greyhounds

I didn't take long to settle in with my family. Like I said, they are easy to get along with. They're very gentle with us, and of course gentleness is welcome in any dog's life. When you've experienced suffering at the hands of people who appear to not know any better, or, as in Ralph's case, deliberate cruelty, then kindness goes a long way towards your healing.

So, my people, they luckily seemed to realize pretty much straight away that we greyhounds have something of a desire to run the show. You'd never regret having any dog in your life, but we greyhounds are a little special and should be treated as thus. I'm not saying we should be treated better than any other dogs in the household. No, of course that would be unfair, it's just that it should be acknowledged that we greyhounds AND any other dogs in our midst, should have the maximum amount of, well, whatever benefit you think might be nice for us greyhounds and our fellow dogs to receive, because we're always very grateful.

Indeed, in my nice new home I finally had the big

collar that had initially smelt of the other dog removed from my neck, and I was given my first very-own collar similar to the one Ralph had. It was beautiful. It had all different shades of yellow and red (although I can't see red as humans see it, so I'll need to trust Clare on that one). The new collar was loose around my neck so it was always comfortable. Apparently it's a house collar, and as I'd never lived in a house before, except for the short time in my foster home, perhaps I'd previously never needed one?

Attached to the collar I had a disc which jingled when I walked. I'd seen those on other dogs but never thought I would ever get one of my own. It's a bit like a badge telling the world of your status. It tells everyone that this dog is being cared for by someone; that she has found her forever home.

Anyway, I loved the collar so much – and my rope was never attached to it because for walks since I've been with my family I've worn a big collar around my body, which, Clare says, is actually known as a harness. These days I no longer wear that pretty collar, though, because for my health I have to wear a different kind of collar which apparently helps to take away my old racing injury pains, but I'll come back to that later.

So, back to the importance of greyhounds. It's true that we greyhounds have been around pretty much in this design for many centuries. Unlike many other dogs, our body and face shape haven't really changed that much. We belong to a group of similar dogs known as sight hounds. This means we see rather well, and it also means that we tend not to miss too much. If someone is trying to sneak a human treat past us without offering us something of equal quality that's suitable for dogs, for example, then we'll let that person know that it's not on to do that, and they should expect some kind of reprisal – a sort of canine uprising. Like a very loud bark, for instance! I have one of those. I'll look the person who has committed the misdemeanor right in the eyes and bark very piercingly, and very loudly. I'm not sure whether other greyhounds do that, or whether it's just something I've taught myself to do in order to get attention, but it generally works.

The origin of greyhounds goes back thousands of years. There is mention, and even some images of us, in texts from Ancient Egypt, Ancient Greece, Turkey and The Middle East. We are also the only breed of dog mentioned in the King James Version of The Bible.

You'll find images of greyhounds in paintings and drawings all across the world, many of which are from three, four, or even five centuries ago (Clare tells me that was a long time ago). Statues have even been created in memory of particular long dogs. There's one on an island off the south coast of England, the Isle of Wight. It's of a dog named Eos who belonged to a man named Prince Albert. He must have been a really important dog that Eos, because there's also a famous painting of him called (simply) *Eos*. There's also a white greyhound on The House of Tudor's coat of arms from five hundred years ago.

Having been bred for our speed, however, has been our downfall, and only those very fast dogs become important to the people who race us. That's why some of us disappear, never to be seen again – including some of the dogs like me who *had been* winning. This is because once we stop being able to win, we're just no use. Hence so many of us spend a lot of time looking for a home which we can call our own, and which will be forever. But, as I'm sure I've made clear, many of us never find that home.

Living in my new (and forever) home when I first arrived, was Clare, her husband, here on in referred to as The Man, and their son, who I shall refer to as The Tall One. In my opinion The Tall One is the greatest human of all – I think it's because he was the one who was around the most when I first arrived. He's very tall, so we sort of match one another. He doesn't live here anymore, though. Clare tells me it's because he has to study and work in another town, but there are times when I miss him. He does come home to see me quite often, and we go to visit him, too, but it's not the same as being with him all the time.

When I first arrived there was a strange creature living in an enclosure in The Tall One's room. The creature was like something I'd never encountered before, and what was even more amazing about him was that he filled his face with food – he absolutely forced as much food into his face as possible. I was astounded that any creature could do that – and even more so because I wanted to know HOW he did it! It was such a good idea. I felt he must have been a very intelligent creature indeed to have thought of it in the first place.

There were also many of those winged creatures living in the area around the house and in the garden at the back of the house. What's more is that they, the people, fed those creatures. This was even though those creatures were perfectly capable of finding their own food. I'd watched them as they sneakily hung around outside and stared in the windows looking as though they were starving to death. Each day they'd do this, right until the food was put out for them – and then once they'd eaten it you'd see them happily waddling off and pulling disgusting wriggling creatures out of the ground, or plucking beasties, seeds, or fruit off plants! Cheeky, that's what those creatures are.

Anyway, enough about those thieving animals, and back to more important canine goings-on. Because of the way in which racing greyhounds are reared together and live in such close proximity to one another, we have that affinity with other greyhounds, but do I understand Ralph? Yes, I think there *are* times when I even understand him. But little did I know as I settled into my home, that on the horizon was another dog I was going to have to contend with – a dog so unlike a greyhound it was a pretty frightening prospect.

Lucy, aka Lucy-Lou, Little-Lou, Luella, Lulu, or even Loopy-Lou (which I don't think is that complimentary really, but I don't think she gets the joke), is an entity all to herself. It's just occurred to me, that those two dogs get an array of names, when I have only two? Peggy or Peg! Hmm, but then when I think about it, I have to admit that I am quite frequently called Beautiful Peg, Pretty Peg, or Gorgeous Girl. All of these names warm my heart. I guess I'd better stop complaining.

So anyway, yes, Lucy!

Lucy – the little dog with the teeth!

Chapter Five

Lucy-Luella-Lou

Lucy's the dog who lived with Clare's mother when I first arrived to live with Clare and the rest of them. The encounters Lucy and I had in the early days were never very positive, in that while she'd clearly learned to tolerate Ralph, she made it clear that she didn't want me around!

She and Ralph had arrived in the family about the same time as one another, and I arrived shortly after that, but you would have thought that I was some great imposter with the way Lucy treated me. We both quite like food treats, and Clare's mother was always one for giving great treats, much to the dismay of Clare. Clare used to classify those treats as being 'unhealthy', but still, her mother kept on giving them to us – usually by sneaking them to us when she thought Clare wasn't looking. But Clare knew, and she would simply shake her head in despair!

Anyway, getting back to the little dog, and she really *is* so very small, especially when compared to Ralph and me. Lucy likes to show her teeth and put up those little hackles, and back in those days she always seemed to target her anger at me. I have to admit that back then I was just a little afraid of her.

There was the time I took a particularly tasty treat from Clare's mother, and Lucy thought it had been for her. I'd been offered, so what was I to do? After all, it would have been impolite of me to refuse. Lucy was NOT happy to say the least, and those hackles came up, and she bared those tiny teeth. You would have thought I had just stolen her whole month's supply of treats. She'd also let me know if I wasn't allowed to stand by Clare's mum, or if I wasn't allowed to touch (or even look at) her toys. I think meeting Lucy was a massive life lesson for me, because that was the first time I'd met a dog who really didn't appear to like me!

Luckily for me, back in those days we didn't encounter one another that often as Clare would often visit there on her own, but little did I know that she would eventually be coming to live with us. Not for some time, though, because for a long time it was just Ralph, the face-filling creature, and me – until eventually the face-filling creature passed away, leaving just Ralph and me.

When I first moved in with Ralph and the family I sensed a sadness in them, so I used to comfort them all. I wondered whether their sadness was to do with the other dogs I could smell traces of in the house. *Don't you worry about those dogs any more*, I used to say to them with my eyes, as I rested my head over someone's arm or across their lap, or wherever they wanted me to rest it. *You've got me now... and Ralph, of course, but he's not so good at the whole comforting humans thing because he needs so much comforting himself, so you'll just have to make do with me.*

And I've noticed they respond, humans do. You simply do that draping head thing and, lo and behold, the hand comes over and they stroke your head, your neck, and down your back. And then they look into your eyes and tell you how lovely you are. Ralph could learn a trick or two from me – he may even find he likes all that human contact after all! Don't get me wrong, he clearly likes having hugs from Clare and the others, even from visitors sometimes, but he doesn't like his head being stroked until he really knows someone. I've never minded who strokes my head; I think it's a great thing! From my racing days I know that many dogs don't ever experience that side of human kindness.

Anyway, enough of Ralph and his woes and back to Lucy. She came to live with us when Clare's mother passed away. One day mine and Ralph's people left the house all upset, and then later on they came back with Lucy the scary dog with the teeth in tow! Again, there was a great sadness in the house and I tried to console them all. This comforting even included (strangely, after all our previous negative encounters) Lucy. She seemed terribly miserable, but despite that she didn't seem too happy about my wanting to help her. In fact, she absolutely wasn't having any of it, and every now and then she would curl her lips at me.

By this time we had moved to another house because Ralph had been frightened of the vehicles on the roads where we used to live, and this new house had a much bigger space outside for us to play in. Unfortunately, when Lucy moved in, this space made Clare panic, because it also gave me much more chasing distance – she was worried I might forget that Lucy was a dog and chase her as though she was a furry creature like the ones I used to chase on the track. Does Clare think I'm stupid or something? Apparently, no, she doesn't think I'm stupid, she says she was simply worried that my greyhound chase-factor instinct would take over if I forgot Lucy was a dog. *Phew, that's okay then*, I thought to myself, *I thought I wasn't allowed to chase her at all – it seems as though as long as I actually acknowledge she's a dog, then it's okay!*

Chapter Six

An Abundance of Greyhounds

We'd established that Lucy was, indeed, a dog. I have to be honest, however, and say that she was, in the early days anyway, a bit of a handful of a dog to contend with. We all certainly needed a settling in period to get to know one another properly. I admit that there were times I wished she would just leave so we could all have our peace and quiet back again, but, no, it seemed as time went by that she was definitely not going anywhere! Clare had apparently been adamant that we would all get on and be one big happy family whatever we dogs thought about it. We had unexpectedly become Lucy's new home to stay in forever, because her last home which had meant to be forever had not been so, through no fault of anyone. I would imagine it was *just one of those things*, as you humans say.

And, anyway, I realized Lucy still seemed to be very sad, and, despite my greyhound chase-factor (as Clare calls it), I secretly felt a bit of empathy for little Lucy. She, Ralph, and me, we all had tough lives before finishing up in a home together, and while there was never a day go by when I didn't think about Roxy and the others, I realized Ralph and Lucy were actually quite nice companions.

When I think back, though, I'm ashamed to admit that I did chase Lucy a couple of times (perhaps a few more, but those are the only times that Clare knows about, and therefore the only ones being recorded here). One time, Clare managed to grab hold of me as I was rushing past her on the trail of Lucy, who, I might add, was actually making me chase her into the garden. Clare's reactions must have been quick, because we greyhounds can certainly move. Meanwhile, Lucy turned, and had she been human I'm sure she would have stuck out her tongue at me. Instead she triumphantly trotted back up towards the house. I could tell she was bluffing, and I think she was actually quite relieved I hadn't caught up with her!

Another time, I actually managed to slip past Clare to catch Lucy, but I didn't grab her or anything – no, not at all, because you know what she did? She turned and looked up at me, and flashed those tiny teeth. I snarled back at her, but then remembered there was a hefty size difference between the two of us, so I left her alone and backed off. Clare, who had been pushing a flowery plant into the ground over on the other side of the garden at the time, had witnessed the whole event. She immediately came over to me and told me I was a good girl. I enjoy good girl moments because they often come laden with good girl food rewards!

I think that event was mine and Lucy's truce moment. Since that day we've not bothered getting cross with one another. We both get a little irritated with Ralph at times, but that's because he's so clumsy. I have never met such a clumsy dog in all my life – and that's coming from a greyhound!

Mind you, when I think about it, he wasn't the one who injured his leg when he put his foot through a gap in a drain cover, and had to go and see the VET for stitches a few Christmases ago. Ralph also wasn't the one who twisted his paw racing in from the back garden (not while chasing Lucy, I might add). And when I ponder over it a little more, I have to acknowledge that Ralph has never been the one who has always got in the way when our people are trying to do something, or when we're trying to maneuver all our dog and human feet around the hall and through the front door to go for a walk.

Nope, that's all yours truly!

Ralph's main clumsiness is associated with his huge

feet! They are everywhere, and when he gets excited he lifts them up and pounds them on the ground like he's some sort of giant prehistoric creature. I don't really know what one of those is, but Clare does, and she said he probably resembles one with those big feet of his. But even those giant feet don't protect him from the wrath of some creatures.

Some time ago, we went on a long walk into town. This was in the days before Lucy came to live with us, so it was just Ralph, The Man, Clare, and little old me. So, there we were, we'd almost arrived at the busiest place in town. We don't normally go up that way because Ralph gets a bit scared of the vehicles, but on that day he was being especially brave. But then, oh my goodness, this huge bird swooped down from the sky and flew in front of us. Clare says they hadn't realized the birds were there, but it seemed they were simply protecting their young. I wonder whether their young looked like Roxy's puppies.

Clare was holding onto Ralph, and she ducked as the bird came flying straight at her. Ralph ducked too, even though he didn't need to. But then, that bird, and another one, came and swooped at them again and Clare screamed. That time, Clare and

Ralph did both need to duck, and Clare threw her arms around Ralph to protect him. When the big birds tried to fly low again, The Man made a loud noise to scare them away. Luckily this time they didn't come back, but Ralph was beside himself with fright, which was a bit of a shame because he'd been doing so well. Anyway, to cut a long story short, Clare and The Man had a discussion, and then they swapped leads so Ralph was with The Man, and he and Ralph headed back home.

With a check overhead for any more dive-bombing creatures of the avian kind, Clare and me, we set off on the rest of our journey. I was a little perturbed that I no longer had Ralph with me – I'd sort of got used to him being my sidekick. I hoped I wasn't on my way to visit the VET, and that the walk hadn't been some way of making me so tired I could be duped into not noticing I was walking into the vet's waiting room!

But then, as Clare and I walked into a clearing on the busy high street, I truly had one of those Greyhound Heaven moments, for there, right in front of us was a lot – an abundance even – of greyhounds. They were all with their people, and just like me they all had on their fancy neck-wear, and were proudly jangling their jingly metal name tags. And, above all else, they all seemed to be happy. We headed down towards the hub of dogs and I greeted them in the familiar, understated way that most of us greyhounds greet one another.

And then, in the crowd, I saw her.

It was Roxy!

She was there with some people. I pulled Clare over so I could greet her. Roxy got excited (again, in that understated way we have), and the two of us sniffed one another and wagged our tails. I was so happy to see her. I wished I could tell Clare that Roxy was my sister, but I had no way of doing that. I was just so happy she was okay – that she, too, had found her way into a forever home. One of her people leaned forward and stroked my head (he seemed nice) and Clare stroked Roxy. If only they had known we were sisters!

After some time, Roxy and her person walked away from us and the rest of the group. I stood and watched her and felt a warm glow in my heart. I was so glad she had found her forever home – so many greyhounds were just not as lucky as we had both been.

That night I lay awake for a long time reflecting on

how life used to be for both of us, and how we'd both come through it all okay and landed on our respective four paws. I wondered whether she had any other dogs to live with. I suspected not, as she had been there on her own, but I like to think she had a Ralph-dog somewhere in her life. Perhaps there was a dog waiting for her back home who'd been scared by the flying creatures, and who'd also been taken away from the pandemonium of the town centre?

Clare says that the day had been all about getting as many rescued greyhounds in town as possible, apparently in order to celebrate the thousand greyhounds who by that point had been rescued by that charity. I'd obviously been one of them, and I imagine that was why it'd been so important for me to attend; Ralph hadn't really needed to be there because he was rescued by a different charity.

And so, when we're rescued we like to thank our people for being so nice to us. Not that we have to, you know. No, nothing like paying back the good deed or anything. It's more of an appreciation thing – and dogs (not only greyhounds) have become the great healers of people. It seems our presence really does help people to feel more relaxed and just generally happier. On the face of it, it would seem that you humans do all the giving and that we're expensive to keep (food, vaccinations, insurance, veterinary treatment, toys, beds etc.), but when you balance it out and consider that human-animal bond thing which Clare is so keen on talking about, we're actually worth every penny!

Chapter Seven

Pet Sitters

Time has passed and we've all learned a lot about one another, humans and dogs alike. When our people aren't working or going to the shops to top up our dog food supplies, we tend to do everything together. We go for walks, we hang about around the house while Clare is working or writing, we relax with them while the noisy box is on in the corner of the room, we go on holidays together, and we're nice to the visitors when they come over.

I have to say that I quite like holidays, because the sea, sand and forest walks do me just fine, and it's nice that they take us with them. I don't like the heat, though. We greyhounds don't do so well in hot weather. No, we'd far rather be lazing in a cool house on one of those large sofas which are designed especially for greyhounds. Three-seaters (or even four) are particularly good because they allow for maximum stretching of the legs.

This year, however, they decided they needed a short holiday – and where they were going they were not able to take us three dogs, which was a bit of an imposition, I felt. But it turns out it wasn't that bad because we were getting a pet sitter. Pet sitters can be fun, because they don't always know all the rules. It transpired, however, that this one was going to be a tough cookie to break. This was because she had what they call 'training'. She had, it seemed, been educated in the ways of we canines. In other words, she wasn't going to be the pushover I'd hoped she'd be.

She clearly knew stuff about dogs, such as to ignore me if I barked at her for more treats. She also knew things like making sure Lucy didn't steal Ralph's food, and to remember to give me my sore leg pills in my dinner. The people think I don't know they hide them there, but I know. Oh yes, I know! I also know that having them in food saves me from having them placed on the back of my tongue and having to have my jaws held closed for ages while they keep on asking me whether or not I've swallowed. Of course I haven't swallowed, I feel like saying, only I can't say that because they've got my mouth closed. And also because I'm a dog.

No, of course we don't swallow when you're holding our heads up and waiting for us to swallow those pills. It's easier to hang on, and then manipulate them around with our tongue and triumphantly spit them out once you let go. But actually those pills somehow seem to help my legs. You know, with those old racing injuries from when I was a youngster I'm in need of a little help, so I'm quite happy to have them 'disguised' (nudge, nudge, wink, wink) in my food.

Talking of food – it would seem that there are still none of those tasty fried sticks (those chip ones I'm not allowed to mention) on the menu – even in this forever home. Even the pet sitter seemed to know this because she wasn't handing any of them to us either. Much as I liked the pet sitter and everything, next time they should find one who loves dogs as much as she clearly does, but who knows nothing about dog behaviour. That would suit me fine – that one simply knew too much for her own good!

Chapter Eight

This Dog Only!

And so, here I am – I've reached the twilight of my life and have become the wise old elder of the group of dogs with whom I share my home. Through my quiet observation of people through the years there is much I've learned, not least that humans and dogs can get on very well together, particularly when the humans are nice ones who treat you well. If there's another thing I've learned on this journey, it's that in this reciprocal human-dog relationship thing that we have going on, *everyone* is a dog whisperer!

Or at least they think they are.

Everyone!

Take Ralph's situation for example. Now it's clear to anyone who knows a thing or two about dogs, that if the person with the dog says, 'Don't touch this dog, but you can stroke her if you like,' (meaning yours truly, of course), then what you must do is remove your approaching hand from going anywhere near Ralph's head, and stroke mine instead. That's because I like such attention, and he doesn't.

So, when our people say that Ralph doesn't like being stroked by people he doesn't know, they really do mean don't touch him. But what do a lot of people do? They say (in human language of course). 'It's okay, dogs like me. I've always loved dogs.'

Then our people, they say something like: 'But Ralph had a tough time before he came to live with us, which has made him extremely head shy, and we think he has bad memories, so please stroke Peggy instead!' At which, they point in my direction. Meanwhile, I'm standing there patiently waiting for the eventual pat on the head, while Ralph backs away from them and makes it obvious he would much rather they came and spoke to me.

In the early days Clare tried training Ralph with treats so he'd know people weren't scary, but back then he'd just about turn himself inside out if anyone approached him, so he was never going to be bribed with food. He's not what they call 'food orientated', you see, and his fears would always override any desire for treats. I think I've already made it clear what I think of treats and, quite frankly, I think Ralph should have just gone with the offers of food. One benefit for me amid all this, however, was that when he refused the treats, I got more.

Anyway, back to dog whispering people. Most of them eventually get the message – unless they're a little drunk or something! Clare said that, not me, because apparently on a few occasions wibbly-wobbly people have stood in front of Ralph trying to stroke him, when they couldn't even stand up properly themselves.

And so, after some debate about whether Ralph likes them or not, in order to gain some personal gratification that dogs *really do* like them despite Ralph's reaction to them, they drift over to me and get the desired response. But inside, I sigh, wishing the walk could be over and we could get back home to the sofa.

Over the last couple of years Lucy has become much more people-friendly. Like Ralph, she used to be a bit frightened of strangers, but now she shares in the love whenever we've been through that whole 'Don't touch Ralph... pleeeeease DON'T... TOUCH... RALPH!' routine.

Not children, though, Clare and the rest of the family still don't let children touch Lucy, even though they're sure she wouldn't hurt anyone. It's mainly because Lucy doesn't like unpredictability and sudden moves which, Clare says, children are sometimes prone to. Me, though, I just love it when children are around – mostly because they always smell of the tasty food they've recently been eating. I also think I like them because they remind me of puppies, in that children behave differently to older people, just like puppies do when compared to older dogs. They're a lot more fun. Lucy wouldn't hurt one (a child, that is, she might growl at a puppy), it's just that Clare and the rest of the family don't want to stress her.

One time shortly after Lucy came to live with us, we were all out for a long walk and we came across a young lad (of about six or seven years old, Clare says) who was out and about playing in the street. His parents weren't anywhere to be seen. He was keen to speak to us three dogs and came rushing over full of enthusiasm. Clare and the man went through the usual routine, with Clare saying to him, 'Do not touch this big dog,' obviously indicating Ralph and not me, 'or this little dog – only touch this big black one.' Meaning me, of course. So I stood there and patiently waited for the nice, small, food-scented hand to come my way.

Just in case he hadn't heard what she'd said to him, Clare repeated, 'Please DON'T TOUCH the little dog!' But then, what did he do? He reached over and touched Lucy on the head. But that wasn't all, for he then immediately turned around to me and pulled my tail. Well, I never! Lucy was really good with him, as was I, but Clare and The Man were not happy that he hadn't followed Clare's instructions.

'I SAID... DON'T... TOUCH... THE LITTLE DOG!' Clare bellowed at him, '... AND DON'T EVER PULL A DOG'S TAIL!' And the boy, now this is what really seemed to make Clare's blood boil, reached over to my face and promptly kissed me on the nose. He then turned to Clare and stuck his tongue out at her. Then he ran off along the road, turning occasionally to stick his fingers up at us! 'AND DON'T KISS STRANGE DOGS EITHER!' Clare called along the street after him.

We never saw that boy again – perhaps he was too frightened to leave the house because of Clare's obvious rage. I doubt it, however, as he didn't seem like a little human who would be frightened of anything – even Clare and all her wrath. Since then there's been a rule that only children who are with their parents are allowed to touch us. Even me, can you believe that? Even me!

The strange thing was, though, that throughout this quite traumatic event, Ralph had just stood there, as calm as anything. It was as though he'd zoned out, as though he'd decided he would prefer to mentally drift into another world in some kind of trance, rather than be a part of the chaos that was going on around him. Meanwhile, Lucy and me, we were simply bewildered. And I have to say, I was just a little perturbed at having had my tail pulled and then having been kissed on the nose. I'd never before in my life ever had my tail pulled and it was quite a distressing experience, I can tell you.

There is one gripe I really must mention here about walks in general. It could be pouring with rain, winds bending the trees to forty-five degrees, snowing, or even bed time, but nothing stops people from partaking in what are apparently known as *The Social Benefits to Humans of Living with Dogs.*

Okay, so we dogs get it that people benefit from the whole concept of spending time outdoors and chatting to the locals in the street whenever we're out for a walk, but we dogs, we happen to find that hanging around with other humans thing rather boring. Unless the people have a dog with them – that makes it a little more interesting. And, of course, as he loves other dogs so much, those are the encounters Ralph prefers. But if there is no dog, or if the dog is one of those boring well-trained ones who don't even acknowledge we're there, then Ralph makes it obvious he doesn't want to stand around waiting while Clare and The Man talk to all and sundry.

Those are the times when Ralph changes his body position so he is dominantly pointing in the direction of home or towards the remainder of our walk, and makes it clear that he thinks the conversation should be OVER. I can't believe that I have just mentioned the words 'dominantly' and 'Ralph' in the same sentence. That dog does not have a dominant bone in his body... I suppose it's lucky we're not wolves then!

Now me, however, in that situation, I would always, without fail, point in the direction of home. While we greyhounds do like a short, sharp burst of exercise, all we really want in life is a comfortable home. And when you get to a home and discover sofas, you realize that is what you've needed your whole life; and that you'd be quite happy to be lying on one pretty much all day every day!

One thing that does provide a little unwelcome exercise is the frightening, noisy thing that our humans push around the house, and which in the early days was something we really were all quite frightened of. I've now got it all worked out, though, because there's a certain strategy to dealing with that machine. All you have to do is stand your ground wherever you are and wait until you see where they are using the machine first. Then, once they've finished that area, you simply move over and position yourself in that place. The machine never comes back. Not until the next time anyway, so you can be pretty sure you're safe.

When I say I have worked this out, I really do mean *I*, because the other two haven't mastered the art of said machine avoidance. They only go and move to an area where the machine hasn't yet been. Of course the machine is going to come and chase you away when you go and stand somewhere that it hasn't yet been. Clare even opens the back door so they have an escape route into the garden but, no, they stick around and end up having to run away from it!

I'm told there are machines like those ones which operate on their own – and it's said they can even work their way around a sleeping dog! I really don't think I would like it if Clare and the others got one of those – I truthfully don't think I could keep my cool with a machine which had a mind of its own.

Chapter Nine

A Greyhound's World

Well I suppose the time has arrived for me to go all philosophical on you all. You know, a bit of a wide-ranging contemplative reflection on life, while I grasp the opportunity to compare that whole forever home thing versus the life of a racing greyhound.

I'm sure I've conveyed that the life of a greyhound being bred to go out onto the tracks is not a good one. There are far more of us born than are ever used to race. This is apparently because the greyhound racing people want to breed the fastest dog of all. Even from an early age some dogs are deemed to be unsuitable to go racing. Those dogs are sometimes found a pet home through a rescue charity – like I have now. Many young dogs, however, like some of those other dogs who have failed on the track because of injury, they just disappear! Never to be seen again. As I mentioned before, some dogs are exported to race on the tracks abroad where the conditions are even worse than they are here.

Quite simply, it is true that many dogs thought to be useless are done away with.

I checked with Clare what we mean by the term *done away with.* She told me we mean killed! I got a big lump in the back of my throat, while a deep throbbing feeling cast a shadow across my chest as I thought of all the greyhounds I'd come across in my life who had simply disappeared. I hoped against hope that they, like me, had found their way to a forever home and had not been *done away with*!

I'm pretty sure I've conveyed earlier on how awful the living conditions are that greyhounds often have to contend with. Some dogs even end up with awful sores on their legs and/or body because they don't have anywhere comfortable to lie down. Those sores can take months to heal – and some of them never do properly heal. I have some bald patches that were once sores: one on my tail and one on the back of my hip bone. They're from the days when I lay on the ground with no comfortable bedding.

When Clare was still working as a veterinary nurse, i.e. when she was actually working with animals, rather than talking about or writing about them all day, she looked after many greyhounds with those deep pressure sores. She says it was heartbreaking seeing those dogs in such a state. Hmm, I can imagine. She and the other nurses had to bathe and dress the wounds sometimes three times a day. She says those greyhounds were all so very brave, but that even after all that intensive treatment, in the end some of them had to be put to sleep because they had other problems from which they never recovered. I'm not so sure what she means by *put to sleep*, either, but it doesn't sound as though it's such a good thing.

Those poor conditions extend into the kennels used for breeding greyhounds for the racing circuits. The kennels are often devoid of anything nice for the dogs, and they are confined to that small space like breeding machines, at the mercy of whoever owns them, I guess. Needless to say, some of the dogs have difficulties when giving birth to their offspring, and then because no one is watching them when the time comes for the puppies to be born, some puppies, and even some bitches, end up dying through lack of care. Some, if they're the runts of the litter, will be disposed of pretty much as soon as it's known they're the weaker ones. I have a horrible feeling *being disposed of* is the same as *being done away with*.

And if we greyhounds make it as far as the tracks, in addition to all our disappearing siblings and other relatives, many dogs are injured while running. Some are hurt really badly so they, too, are put to sleep. There's that term again – this is really worrying. Who'd want to be a racing greyhound?

It sometimes takes a long time for the vet to get to the injured dog because, even in this day and age, there are some tracks that still don't have a VET on site when there's a race going on. Some owners, even though they've been making money from racing the dog, when the dog is injured they don't want to pay for treatment, and it's easier (for them) to do that 'doing away' with the dog thing, even if the dog's injury could have been treated.

Even those who have lesser injuries, like I did, immediately become no use for running because we'd be far too slow. A racing greyhound has to be fast, or we're just no good. We become waste that falls by the wayside, sometimes never to be seen again.

Vanish! Just like that!

There's a lot of cheating that goes on, too, with dogs being given injections which make them build up muscle, which then makes them run faster. It's said that some dogs are hobbled in some way (like

Rex with the sticky stuff between his toes), so they *don't* win. It's as though these people don't seem to know what they're doing. Do they want us to be fast, or don't they? Clare tells me it's all about the stakes, and how much money is placed on the dogs. It might be in a person's interests to make the dog slower so they don't win when they had been expected to. I have to say it all sounds highly confusing and very unjust to me.

It's not only we dogs who suffer at the hands of an industry which clearly exploits us so much. Some people also suffer, especially some of those who bet money on which dog might win. The clue is in the word *might* there, as there's no guarantee that *any* dog will win. Gambling on races can apparently lead to many problems for that person – for example a lot of debt (I don't know what that is but it sounds very serious), family break-down (that doesn't sound so good either), and addiction. I think addiction is like that thing I have to certain treats like our new spinach and kale ones. Clare has corrected me, because apparently in this case addiction is a severe psychological problem, and not simply a desire to have a constant supply of the tastiest treats in the world. (Like those 'not allowed' tasty chips which I'm not allowed to mention, for instance).

So, barring the absence of any of those aforementioned tasty chip treats that some humans eat, homes that are forever ones, which are nice and comfy with kind people, that sort of life is certainly the best kind.

I've recently been given the special collar I mentioned. It has a magnet inside which some people believe helps dogs who are in pain. They apparently help some people too (bracelets though, not collars – a bracelet wouldn't be any good for a dog, because it would fall off). Anyway, people thought they'd try them on our canine neck wear as well. I have mine and I think it probably does help me a little with my old racing injuries, along with those special anti-inflammatory pills from the vet, of course. Clare says the collar did seem to help as soon as they put it on me, and they leave it on me just in case it is helping. They also sneak some special oil capsules into my food, but just like my pills from the vet – I KNOW they're there!

The other benefits of being in a home are obviously vast – but I guess that above all else it's nice to be with people and dogs and not having to run, not having to be shut away in a kennel, and not having to be in vehicles on the road all the time between races. It's also particularly nice knowing that this is *my* family – my family for keeps.

Chapter Ten

My Comrades and Me

Despite the pills I'm feeling my age now. I feel it in my joints, and in my muscles and bones. The old ticker is still going well, which is a good thing, and the vets say I'm in good condition for an old greyhound. I still like to think of myself as being that young thing, back when I was able to run without being sore. We greyhounds certainly like to run, but we really don't appreciate being forced into running. That whole thing about racing dog against dog is really not good, and we certainly don't appreciate some of the things that go on at the tracks. Let dogs run for fun, and absolutely not for sport. It's really fun to run, but it's really not sport-like to make dogs run when perhaps they don't want to.

I wish my time had always been in a home that was forever, with sofas and a noisy box in the corner that's sometimes on too loud, walks by the water, holidays, cold winter nights lying by the fire, and just lots of relaxing time. If my life had always been that way, then I truly would have been a lucky girl.

Ralph has a curly-coated buddy named Buster-dog. Personally I can take him or leave him, but Ralph and Buster get on very well together, so well that it can be quite embarrassing when they greet one another and leap about all over the place. Lucy, however, detests Buster, but I imagine that's those terrier ways of hers that I've come to respect. Buster's had his lovely forever home since he was very young, and that must be a really nice thing for a dog.

I guess I was lucky ending up in a home where I had some fellow canine company. I really have come to appreciate them both over these years. I think, though, that sometimes I miss greyhound company and it might have been nice if I'd been in a house with another greyhound, especially if Roxy and I could have been together. But overall I think I've got over that *only greyhounds will do* exclusivity attitude.

I think after all that Ralph really *is* a nearly-greyhound, it's just he has a few traits that are a little otherworldly (non-greyhound). I've tried to understand why he is the way he is. I know it's not his fault, it's just that some humans don't understand the needs of us dogs, and perhaps the people who had him before shouldn't have had a dog to begin with. People who hurt animals, like he's clearly been hurt, they don't deserve to have the privilege of living with a dog.

The three of us, we've managed to reach a state where we're all content with our life here. Clare and the others seem happy to have us around – apparently that's all part of that thing I mentioned called the human-animal bond, in that we all derive some emotional and social benefits from being with one another. I don't know what it is, but it feels nice.

I know that when they go out for a few hours I miss them, I also miss them when we have to have one of those pet sitters come to stay. As much as pet sitters are nice and all, I really wouldn't want them to stay forever. Whenever our people have been out and they return, I feel so happy that I grab one of those toys of mine and take it to show them. That's the most excited I ever really get. And my people's reaction? They seem to get excited when they see me greet them with one of my puppy toys in my mouth, and they say to me 'Peggy, you're so clever!'

Clare thinks I must have always wanted to have had my own puppies, and that's why I do all these strange maternal things like nesting and always carrying toys as though they are puppies. Knowing what I know now about homeless dogs, though, it's perhaps a good thing I didn't ever have any. What would have become of them all? Would they, too, have disappeared into the vast void of missing greyhounds? Who knows? Is the answer to that question. Clare tells me it's okay to sometimes answer a question with a question, because for some questions there really are no answers, and we can only speculate. I'm sure that makes sense to some of you, but it's a bit much for me, so I'll just go with it and trust she's right.

Finally, I just want to express that, while all dogs are actually good companions for humans (but only some humans good companions for dogs), there are some dogs who may suit some humans better than others. If you like a fairly easy life with a dog who is happy to just be around you, then definitely consider rescuing a greyhound. If you're after a more exciting life, then there are lots of dogs out there who are a bit more demanding, dogs like Lucy, I suppose. And, quite frankly, some dogs demand more attention than others do. I have one dog in mind when I say that: there's a squashed face lunatic big dog who lives nearby.

Because he was new to the area, we'd never met him before the fateful day I'm going to tell you about, but one day some time ago, he was barking from his living room as we were taking a gentle walk past his house. Minding our own business we were, but there he was, woofing at the top of his voice through his downstairs living room window. Now, it was quite a warm day, but not too hot otherwise we'd have been at home. We don't go out when it's too hot because it makes us pant... sorry, I digress.

Anyway, so there we were, quietly having a sniff at the trees as we walked past his house, when there was suddenly a loud rumpus of urgent barking coming through the window – I'd never heard such an excitable racket. Because it was warm outside, the window to his house was a little way open. Well, then, who'd have thought it, but the dog suddenly appeared right in front of us! He'd flown out of the window, just like those annoying flying creatures, and had landed right in front of us. We were almost nose to nose and he was staring right at me with his large eyes, and wagging his long tail!

I imagine he only wanted to say hello to his new local fellow canines, but I had such a shock when he appeared there like that! I'd never seen such a thing in my life. Lucy, of course, wanted to bite him, and Ralph, who would normally have wanted to play with a new dog, was just a little perturbed at the sight of this dog who could fly out of windows!

The big, squashed face dog's person came running outside to fetch him – he hadn't known he could do that flying thing. Those dogs must be more intelligent than I give them credit for! Anyway, once the flying dog was taken back inside and we resumed our walk, Clare and The Man laughed all the way home – I wasn't sure what they thought was so funny, as it really had been quite traumatic! I shall never understand these humans, or non-greyhounds for that matter.

Finally, before I finish, I have a very important piece of advice for other dogs (all dogs this time, not only greyhounds), and take heed, because this is very, very important!

Now concentrate very carefully... if you can avoid it, don't go and live with a human who is a veterinary nurse! Honestly, they are so smothering. If you even dare to rub your face along the ground because you have a bit of an itch and it's the easiest way to scratch it, for example, then your mouth gets opened and your teeth and gums examined. If you rub your ear or scratch at it, there is an immediate examination deep inside your ear, and sometimes a horrible cold fluid is squirted deep into your ear canal, closely followed by a rub (although I quite like the rubbing part). And if you have the tiniest blemish on your skin, it's examined and a bit of fur clipped away, apparently so it can be observed over the days and nights that follow. Honestly, you can't even have an itchy behind or lick your what-not without her checking under your tail. So, anyway, this is a message for Clare: just back off, I'll let you know if there's actually something wrong. Okay?

Apparently that's not okay.

Hmm, in that case I imagine all I have left to say, and this is for my human readers now, is that if you have a little spare love in your heart, consider enhancing your life by giving one of us greyhounds a nice home. Go on, you too could have a dog just like me. Or perhaps you'd prefer a rescued non-greyhound? That's okay, too, because of course the key is in the word 'rescued'.

And it's a deal, if you rescue us, we'll rescue you back. It's all part of that human-dog bond thing.

I'm sure you won't regret it! Happy rescued days to

you all! Peggy

Final Thoughts - Clare

I truly hope I have done Peggy justice and reflected through this story how she is. If I have portrayed a wise old dog with a gentle, seemingly considerate nature, and, of course, a healthy appetite, then I have achieved what I set out to achieve.

On this beautiful spring day, the French doors are open from the living room into the garden and she is happily pottering around out there. Earlier, she made me laugh as she trotted curiously towards a wood pigeon, and then immediately looked up in wonder as the pigeon fluttered away. She won't stay out there for long as she's not keen on the heat, instead she'll come back inside and head up to the coolest part of the house on the landing.

For much of her story here, Peggy is the observer: the onlooker of the cruelty that happens in the world of racing. Later, she becomes the participant in the changes that happen once she has been handed over to rescue. She has clearly been one of the luckier ones, as so many, many dogs fall by the wayside and don't ever experience a loving home.

Greyhound racing is clearly wrong – on the most basic level dogs are being forced into breeding and running, and then eventually it is the luck of the draw whether an individual dog sees a life beyond racing.

Peggy is slowing down, but every time we think she seems to be showing her age, she'll do something like chase Ralph or Lucy in from the garden (overtaking them, of course, even at her age). Other times, she'll stand and bark at us until we go and fetch her a treat. Yes, embarrassingly, even with my many years of training I let my dogs get away with bossing me around!

We are lucky to have her and, honestly, if you have a space in your life for a dog, a dog just like Peggy would fill your heart with joy.

Buddies

OTHER BOOKS BY CLARE COGBILL

A Dog Like Ralph

... A Book for Anyone Who has Ever Loved a Rescue Dog

The true story of Ralph—a rescue dog with a difficult past who loves other dogs, is frightened of people and cars, and mesmerized by cats, rabbits and 'Santa Please Stop Here' signs. Clare, his new human, tells with equal amounts of joy and sadness of the challenges and delights of having him as a companion.

His story is partly told through his eyes and describes how what he may have experienced before has affected how he interacts with those in his new 'forever' home. When Ralph's compatriots, Peggy and Luella (Lucy to her friends), enter his life, it becomes clear that they have their own 'version of events' to add to the story!

Clare also writes about the pitfalls of a society that has resulted in Ralph being the way he is, and of how small changes could transform the plight of abandoned dogs. This book is a tribute to the rescue dog.

A Dog Like Ralph gives some of the back story to *The Diary of a Human and a Dog (or Three)* and *A Dog Like Peggy,* but it is not necessary to read either book first.

The Diary of a Human and a Dog (or Three)

The story of a human and a dog sharing their unanticipated grief

When a dog loses their human companion it results in the upheaval of everything they've ever loved. When a human loses their parent it is the most heart-rending thing to have to deal with.

Lucy had been rescued just three years earlier and had spent that time living as the sole dog in charge of an old woman. When the old woman passed away, Lucy found herself thrust into a life in which she would have to share her new humans with two other dogs. She'd encountered Ralph and Peggy before and, quite frankly and in her stroppy terrier way, was not that keen on them.

This is the diary of Clare and Lucy. It is a story of how dogs can help humans heal, and how humans can help dogs to overcome their own very special sort of grief.

This book is Clare's most personal book as it focuses not only on the way in which grief can affect us, but more importantly, on how dogs and people can help one another along the road to recovery. She wrote it in the year following her mother's unexpected death, and it fills the gap between *A Dog Like Ralph* and *A Dog Like Peggy*.

A Soldier Like Jack

Like millions of other young men, Jack was plunged into a war which was to change his life, and the lives of his loved ones, forever. Jack's war would take him to Salonika (Thessaloniki), in Greece. His two brothers were sent to fight on The Western Front.

Jack's wife, Grace, narrates the harrowing true story of what happened to the men, and the families they left behind. It traces their lives from the time of Jack and Grace's marriage in 1912, until Grace's death in 1957.

This is a true story based on the lives of the author's great grandparents, Jack and Grace Cogbill.

Clare wrote this book after feeling touched by a story she came across when embarking on the genealogy of her family. This story is the reason Clare chose the name Cogbill as her pen name: in honour of the three Cogbill men in her family who lost their lives as a result of The Great War.

Lilac Haze

You don't remember your childhood in detail, so your memories thirty or forty years on become hazy; times you had back then are painted in images that have become distorted.

This is a love story. In the end, anyway, that's what it will be. A love story gives you hope: whatever you've lost; whatever you have to gain. For me, as someone on daily kidney dialysis, when an offer of a kidney came along which I couldn't possibly refuse, there was everything to gain.

But the past has a way of interfering with what seems to be the right path... and how do you ever in this life repay such an immeasurable debt?

Clare wrote this book because of her own experience of losing her father to kidney failure in 1970, and then going on to receive her husband's kidney in 2002 after her own kidneys had failed.

Vegan Cookbook

Delicious soups, tempting starters, wholesome main courses, naughty and nice sweet treats. More than 100 tried and tested recipes for you and your friends to enjoy... vegans and non-vegans alike.

These recipes are nutritious, fun, easy, and naturally free from dairy and eggs, and all other animal products.

Clare became vegetarian in 1977 and has been vegan since 2002. Her whole family is vegan and these are some of their most-loved dishes.

The Indie Gluten Free Vegan

Following her husband's coeliac disease diagnosis, Clare revisited many of the recipes in her vegan cook book and created more, all for this 100% vegan gluten free cookbook.

The book includes 120 recipes – soups, suppers and sweets.

If you've enjoyed any of my books, do please get in touch through Facebook or Goodreads.

Reviews on Amazon and/or ratings on Goodreads are very gratefully received.

Thank you so much for reading my books.

Clare

ABOUT THE AUTHOR

Clare Cogbill was born in the mid-1960s, and like many youngsters from an early age she developed a deep passion for animals and their welfare. She had fifteen years experience of working with domesticated animals in rescue shelters, and as a qualified veterinary nurse in both welfare and private practice environments before, in 1991, becoming a lecturer in animal care and veterinary nursing. These days she mostly teaches companion animal welfare, and wild and companion animal behaviour.

While animals have always been her greatest interest, she also loves to read, preferring biographies to fiction, and where those books contain some reference to the human-animal bond, all the better. She also enjoys reading books that have been made into films, but still can't quite work out whether it's better to read the book or to see the film first!

Clare has one son who has now flown the nest and is following his own dreams. She lives in Scotland with her husband and three rescue dogs: Ralph, Peggy and Lucy-Lou.

A Dog Like Peggy

The Life and Times of a Rescued Greyhound

Clare Cogbill has asserted her right under the Copyright, Designs and Patents Act 1988 to be identified as the author of this work.

This book is sold subject to the condition that it shall not, by way of trade or otherwise, be lent, resold, hired out, or otherwise circulated without the author's prior consent.

Locations or the names of individuals have been changed where requested to protect the identity of those people, and in this case dogs too. Any likeness to others (human or canine) is purely coincidental.

This book is not intended as a veterinary text or a source of advice to anyone regarding their animal's health or behaviour. It is the author's personal expression of events as they occurred, and from Peggy's racing days, to reflect the life of a racing greyhound, not necessarily Peggy. The people described through the racing section of this book are fictitious and bear no known similarity to the people Peggy may have encountered. Any resemblance is purely accidental. The author accepts no responsibility for how others may interpret her work.

A Dog Like Peggy

A Dog Like Peggy

A Dog Like Peggy

Printed in Great Britain
by Amazon